Robert F. Bruner
Robert M. Conroy, CFA
Wei Li
Elizabeth F. O'Halloran
Miguel Palacios Lleras
Darden Graduate School
of Business Administration
University of Virginia

Investing in Emerging Markets

The Research Foundation of AIMR™

Research Foundation Publications

Investing in Emerging Markets

ISBN 0-943205-64-6

Printed in the United States of America

August 12, 2003

Editorial Staff
Roger Mitchell
Book Editor

Rebecca L. Bowman	Jaynee M. Dudley
Assistant Editor	Production Manager
Kelly T. Bruton/Lois A. Carrier	Kara H. Morris
Production and Composition	Online Production

Mission

The Research Foundation's mission is to encourage education for investment practitioners worldwide and to fund, publish, and distribute relevant research.

Biographies

Robert F. Bruner is Distinguished Professor of Business Administration and executive director of the Batten Institute at the Darden Graduate School of Business Administration, University of Virginia. He has written about emerging markets, mergers and acquisitions, corporate finance, and corporate transformation.

Robert M. Conroy, CFA, is Paul Tudor Jones II Research Professor of Business Administration at the Darden Graduate School of Business Administration, University of Virginia. He has published articles and case studies on valuation, derivatives, and the microstructure of capital markets. Much of Professor Conroy's recent research has focused on Japanese financial markets.

Wei Li is associate professor of business administration at the Darden Graduate School of Business Administration, University of Virginia. His research and publications focus on public finance, taxation, industrial organization, international economics, the Chinese economy and economic reform in China, and emerging markets finance.

Elizabeth F. O'Halloran is director of intellectual capital at the Batten Institute, University of Virginia, where she leads the development of new knowledge supported by the Institute. Her recent projects have focused on emerging markets, knowledge transfer, cross-border foundations of entrepreneurship, and corporate innovation.

Miguel Palacios Lleras is a fellow at the Batten Institute, University of Virginia. His research has focused on the design of new financial instruments, liquidity and control premiums, assessment of real options in the presence of uncertainty, and human capital finance. He is the author of *Investing in Human Capital* and other related articles.

Contents

Foreword

In May 2002, the Research Foundation of the Association for Investment Management and Research™, in partnership with the Batten Institute at the Darden Graduate School of Business Administration of the University of Virginia and the prestigious finance journal *Emerging Markets Review*, cosponsored a two-and-a-half-day conference on "Valuation in Emerging Markets." This event brought together leading academics and practitioners from around the world to present research and to exchange ideas, resulting in a discourse that leveraged both the rigor of academia and the practical experience and insights of leading investment practitioners. The Research Foundation recognized the importance of capturing and preserving this wealth of knowledge and thus enthusiastically encouraged the development of this Research Foundation monograph.

Robert F. Bruner, Robert M. Conroy, CFA, Wei Li, Elizabeth F. O'Halloran, and Miguel Palacios Lleras have produced an outstanding document that extends far beyond a summary of the conference's papers and presentations. They have arranged the contents of the conference into a cohesive collection of chapters, adding where necessary supplementary data and information that was not explicitly presented or discussed by the conference's participants. Moreover, the authors have brought their own considerable expertise to bear on the subject, resulting in an even richer collection of knowledge filtered through a prism that focuses it on the very real challenges faced every day by investors in emerging markets.

For example, they describe the essential features that distinguish emerging markets from developed markets. They provide a statistical summary of the return and risk attributes of emerging markets. They test the efficiency of emerging markets. They evaluate the degree of integration among emerging markets. And finally, they provide an extensive review of valuation methods applied to emerging market securities.

Their analysis provides valuable insights about appropriate allocation to emerging markets within broad portfolios, the choice of active or passive management, the relative importance of country and sector stratification, the optimal currency exposure, and the efficacy of fundamental and quantitative analysis.

This monograph is clearly an invaluable resource for those who invest in emerging markets, yet it serves a more important purpose. By shining a light on a region of the world that is not well understood by most investors and often neglected, the authors promote prudent investment in economies that are in most need of external funding. And by synthesizing and disseminating the collected wisdom of the leading scholars and practitioners who gathered in Charlottesville, they help to extend the application of best practices to emerging markets.

The Research Foundation is proud to present *Investing in Emerging Markets*.

Mark Kritzman, CFA
Research Director
The Research Foundation of the
Association for Investment Management and Research

Preface

The large number of investment valuation practices for securities in emerging markets and the volatility of their returns make the focus of this Research Foundation monograph timely and important. There is no clear "best practice" for the valuation of assets and securities in emerging markets, although there may be many "worst practices." Our aim in this monograph is to illuminate the issues in a way that helps practicing securities analysts and portfolio managers adopt sensible approaches. This monograph summarizes the wide range of considerations facing investors in these markets. It also recommends approaches to guide investors in adopting appropriate responses for particular circumstances.

This topic is important because the investment flows into emerging markets are material: According to the World Bank, in 2000, portfolio and foreign direct investment flows into the approximately 30 markets classified as emerging topped $250 billion. Although small in comparison with investment flows within and among developed markets, these flows are large enough that improved valuation practices could have a significant effect on investors' wealth.

Today, investment flows into emerging markets are in a cyclical investment trough, but many analysts and portfolio managers see a rising secular trend. Thus, how to thoughtfully assess the risk and value evident in these markets will be of enduring concern to analysts and fund managers around the world. At present, even writers of textbooks disagree about fundamental issues, such as estimating the cost of capital for discounting cash flows in emerging markets. For reasons outlined in this monograph, the dynamic socioeconomic state of these countries will provide an ongoing challenge to securities analysts charged with investing in emerging markets.

The concept for this monograph grew out of the conference "Valuation in Emerging Markets," hosted in May 2002 by the Batten Institute at the Darden Graduate School of Business Administration of the University of Virginia, in partnership with *Emerging Markets Review* and the Research Foundation of the Association for Investment Management and Research. The hosts sought to present both high-quality and highly accessible theoretical and applied research on emerging markets and are grateful for the support of the many participants who helped explore the issues.

The conference keynote speaker, Campbell Harvey, and featured speakers Michael Duffy, Vihang Errunza, Marc Faber, Kristen Forbes, George Houget, Mehran Nakhjavani, Mark Mobius, and Mark Zenner assessed how emerging markets differ from developed ones in areas such as accounting transparency, cost of capital, liquidity, corruption, volatility, governance, taxes, and transaction costs. These issues also were discussed by those who presented papers at the conference: Ervin Black and Thomas Carne, Hoyt Bleakley, Bernard Dumas, Alexander Dyck, Javier Estrada, Kenneth Froot and Jessica Tjornhom, R. Gaston Gelos, Jack Glenn, Kent Hargis, Leora Klapper and Inessa Love, Kai Li, Darius Miller, David Ng, Sandeep Patel, Luis Pereiro, Ana Paula Serra, Amadou Sy, Ignacio Vélez-Pareja, and Peter Wysocki. Their comments and reflections served as a basis for many of the insights articulated in this monograph. In carrying forward their work, we hope that this monograph elucidates the major issues, advances the discussion around valuation, and affords a useful lens through which to observe future development in emerging markets.

We thank Javier Estrada for his counsel on the development of this monograph and of the emerging markets conferences, which are now an annual event at the Batten Institute. Likewise, we gratefully acknowledge the financial support of the Batten Institute and the Trustees of the University of Virginia Darden School Foundation. Last but not least, we give thanks to our families and friends in the Darden community without whose support and encouragement this monograph would not have been possible. The contributions of these people notwithstanding, this monograph may not reflect their views—we alone remain responsible for its contents.

Robert F. Bruner
Robert M. Conroy, CFA
Wei Li
Elizabeth F. O'Halloran
Miguel Palacios Lleras
University of Virginia
May 2003

1. Introduction

Approximately 30 markets are considered to be in transition to higher levels of economic development, and these markets have been widely followed by the international investment community. The International Finance Corporation (IFC) of the World Bank coined the term "emerging financial markets" to refer to the set of countries for which it had begun to calculate stock market indexes. As these markets developed during the 1980s and 1990s, they became more attractive to investors. Initially, in 1981, the IFC's series of emerging market indexes included only 9 countries; by 2002, the total number of countries had reached 33. [1] (Standard & Poor's acquired the IFC indexes in January 2000. Since then, the indexes have been called the S&P/IFC indexes). The Morgan Stanley Capital International (MSCI) Emerging Market Free (EMF) Index provides the other major listing of emerging markets and includes stock markets in a total of 26 countries.[2] The countries identified as emerging markets by the S&P/IFC Investable Composite Index and MSCI EMF indexes are shown in **Table 1.1**. Because the S&P/IFC indexes include the broadest set of countries, they are used in this monograph. In addition to classifying markets as emerging, S&P also publishes indexes for less-developed, or "frontier," markets.[3]

Before 1980, net private portfolio investment to emerging markets was negligible because of the lack of available instruments in which foreign investors could invest and the perceived high-risk volatility of these markets. Beginning in 1981, such investment in the emerging markets started to grow. In 1989, fueled by financial liberalization in many emerging markets, net private portfolio investment surpassed the US$10 billion mark for the first time (rising to US$14.9 billion). This year also saw the beginning of the IFC Investable (IFCI) indexes, which track emerging market stocks that are both legally and practically available to foreign investors.

---

[1] Greece and Portugal were included in the list but were recently reclassified as developed markets.

[2] A more thorough discussion of the indexes is provided in Chapter 2.

[3] The S&P/IFC frontier markets are Bangladesh, Ecuador, Latvia, Romania, Botswana, Estonia, Lebanon, Slovenia, Bulgaria, Ghana, Lithuania, Trinidad and Tobago, Cote d'Ivoire, Jamaica, Mauritius, Tunisia, Croatia, Kenya, Namibia, and Ukraine.

Table 1.1. Emerging Market Countries Included in S&P/IFCI and MSCI EMF Indexes

Country	S&P/IFC	MSCI EMF
Argentina	×	×
Bahrain	×	
Brazil	×	×
Chile	×	×
China	×	×
Colombia	×	×
Czech Republic	×	×
Egypt	×	×
Hungary	×	×
India	×	×
Indonesia	×	×
Israel	×	×
Jordan	×	×
Malaysia	×	×
Mexico	×	×
Morocco	×	
Nigeria	×	
Oman	×	
Pakistan	×	×
Peru	×	×
Philippines	×	×
Poland	×	×
Russia	×	×
Saudi Arabia	×	
Slovakia	×	
South Africa	×	×
South Korea	×	×
Sri Lanka	×	
Taiwan	×	×
Thailand	×	×
Turkey	×	×
Venezuela	×	×
Zimbabwe	×	×
Total	33	26

Source: Standard & Poor's Emerging Markets Data Base (S&P's EMDB) and DataStream.

During the first half of the 1990s, the privatization and economic liberalization that took place in many emerging market countries created a strong catalyst for investment. Net private portfolio inflows to emerging markets peaked in 1994 at US$113 billion, only to decrease sharply in the following years, mainly as a result of the widespread financial turmoil that affected these markets. **Figure 1.1** shows a strong relationship between net portfolio investment and total return on the S&P/IFCI Composite Index. Both portfolio investment and the S&P/IFCI Composite Index's total return decreased sharply during the Mexican crisis in 1995 and after the Asian and Russian crises in 1997 and 1998.

The combination of rapid growth of investment opportunities and higher volatility in emerging markets raises fundamental questions for investors about how to incorporate emerging markets in the overall investment process:

- Should emerging market portfolios be managed actively or passively?
- Should portfolio decisions be based more on country or industry sector factors?
- Should investors hedge away currency risk?

Figure 1.1. Net Portfolio Investment in Emerging Markets and Performance of the S&P/IFCI Composite Index, 1980–2003

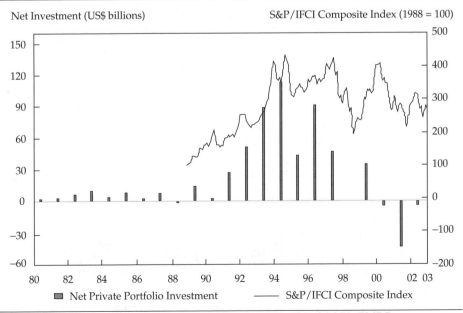

Source: Based on data from the International Monetary Fund and S&P's EMDB.

- Should individual investments be selected based on fundamental analysis or quantitative models?

Any insight about these questions depends on the various characteristics of emerging markets, including past performance, market efficiency, and global integration. It also depends on the fundamental question of how to value emerging market securities. Although the investment opportunities that these markets offer should require the use of valuation techniques that take into account the particularities of these markets, there is no consensus on an appropriate valuation model. Indeed, a single model is unlikely ever to exist because of great variation in the quality and availability of information and the integration among emerging markets. This monograph examines the relevant differences among these markets and analyzes the applicability of various valuation models for emerging markets.

Providing such analysis for valuation in emerging markets is important for at least four reasons. First, no clear "best practice" exists for the valuation of assets and securities in emerging markets. In developed markets, practitioners and scholars seem to converge on mainstream valuation practices; see, for example, Bruner, Eades, Harris, and Higgins (1998) and Graham and Harvey (2001), which document a clustering of practices around tools and concepts of modern finance. In emerging markets, valuation methodology varies much more widely, as shown in surveys in Bohm et al. (2000) and Pereiro (2002). Even among the writers of textbooks, substantial disagreement exists about fundamental issues, such as estimating the cost of capital.

Second, emerging markets differ from developed markets in areas such as accounting transparency, liquidity, corruption, volatility, governance, taxes, and transaction costs. Such differences are quite likely to affect valuation. In fact, several researchers have argued that these issues have significant economic implications and warrant careful consideration in the application of valuation approaches.

Third, investment flows to emerging markets are material: Although dwarfed by investment flows within and among developed markets, emerging market inflows are large enough that improved valuation practices could have a material impact on the welfare of investors and their targeted investments. Also not to be ignored is a humanitarian consideration: Better valuation practices may enhance the flow of investment capital and the allocation of resources, thereby increasing the social welfare of emerging market populaces.

Fourth, emerging markets will continue to draw the attention of the world's investors. The rate of economic growth in these markets is often two or three times faster than in developed countries. The roughly 150 countries not regarded as developed account for a predominant share of the global population, landmass, and natural resources. A premise of the diplomatic policies of most developed countries is that ties of trade and investment will help draw emerging market countries into a more stable web of international relations.

2. Characteristics of Emerging Markets

Investors should be concerned with two important underlying assumptions when valuing assets in emerging markets—the information available about the investment and the risk of the investment relative to global markets. Chapters 2, 3, and 4 address various aspects of information (basic characteristics of emerging markets; diversification, return, and volatility; and market efficiency), and Chapter 5 elaborates on the issues associated with comparative investment risk.

Within emerging markets, the size, transparency, and liquidity of a market yield important clues as to the state and accessibility of relevant data within a particular country. The information found in small, illiquid, and information-ally "opaque" markets is much less likely to reveal information about prices and market expectations than is the information found in large, liquid, and transparent ones. Because the financial and socioeconomic infrastructures of the approximately 30 emerging markets are dramatically varied, the quality and amount of available information also varies among them.

Defining Emerging Markets

Emerging markets form the tier of economies just below the developed economies. This definition, however, is too broad. The S&P/IFC indexes consider a market "emerging" if it meets at least one of the following two criteria:[1]

- It is a low-, lower-middle, or upper-middle-income economy as defined by the World Bank.
- Its investable market capitalization[2] is low relative to its most recent GDP figures.

In contrast, S&P/IFC defines[3] a market as "developed" if it meets both of the following conditions:

- GNP per capita exceeds the World Bank's upper-middle-income threshold for at least three consecutive years. (In 2000, the threshold was $9,266.)
- The investable market-cap-to-GDP ratio is in the top 25 percent of the emerging market universe for three consecutive years.

---

[1]Standard & Poor's (2000), p. 2.

[2]Investable market capitalization is the market capitalization after removing holdings not available to foreign investors.

[3]Standard and Poor's (2000), p. 2.

Exhibit 2.1 shows how the countries fit into the World Bank's income categories, with the countries included in the S&P/IFC emerging market indexes highlighted in bold text. With more than 150 countries in the low-, lower-middle-, and upper-middle-income groups and only 32 classified as emerging markets, S&P/IFC indexes clearly use criteria other than income level to categorize countries into developed, emerging, frontier, and unclassified markets. These other criteria involve issues related to macroeconomic characteristics, size of markets, liquidity, and corruption. In a broad sense, these are exactly the same characteristics that investors need to consider when they invest in an emerging market.

Macroeconomic Characteristics. Emerging markets have higher levels of income and financial market depth than frontier markets. **Table 2.1** shows the market cap, GDP, and GNP per capita for the countries included in the S&P/IFC emerging market indexes. **Figure 2.1** highlights the significance of income and financial market depth (ratio of market cap to GDP) for 70 countries categorized as emerging and frontier markets by S&P/IFC.[4] Not surprisingly, markets designated as emerging tend to have a higher ratio than those designated as frontier. When *investable* market cap is used, the disparity between the two groups becomes even greater.

Emerging market countries have lower GNP per capita and lower investable market cap relative to developed markets, as indicated by a comparison of Table 2.1 and **Table 2.2**. For example, in 1999, the United States had a GNP per capita[5] of $31,910 and a ratio of market cap to GDP of approximately 1.47. Malaysia, an emerging market during this period, had a GNP per capita of $3,390 and a ratio of market cap to GDP of about 1.25. When the investable market cap is used, the ratio is closer to 0.33.

Figure 2.2 shows a comparison of emerging markets and developed markets on the basis of GNP per capita and the ratio of market cap to GDP for 1999. The difference between the emerging and developed markets is much greater than between frontier and emerging markets. The two emerging markets closest to being reclassified to developed markets are Israel, with a GNP per capita of $16,310 and a market-cap-to-GDP ratio of 0.39, and South Korea, with a GNP per capita of $8,490 and a market-cap-to-GDP ratio of 0.28.

---

[4]Of the sample, S&P/IFC classified 32 of the countries as emerging markets, 19 as frontier markets, and 19 as unclassified. Because investable market cap was not available for the frontier markets, total market cap was used instead.

[5]International Finance Corporation (1998).

Exhibit 2.1. World Bank Income Classifications for the Year 2000
(S&P/IFC emerging market countries shown in bold)

Low-income economics (63)—GNP per capita US$755 or less

Afghanistan	Central African	Ghana	Madagascar	**Nigeria**	Tanzania
Angola	Republic	Guinea	Malawi	North Korea	Togo
Armenia	Chad	Guinea-Bissau	Mali	**Pakistan**	Uganda
Azerbaijan	Comoros	Haiti	Mauritania	Rwanda	Ukraine
Bangladesh	Congo (Dem. Rep.)	**India**	Moldova	Sao Tome	Uzbekistan
Benin	Congo (Rep.)	**Indonesia**	Mongolia	Senegal	Vietnam
Bhutan	Cote d'Ivoire	Kenya	Mozambique	Sierra Leone	Yemen
Burkina Faso	Eritrea	Kyrgyz	Myanmar	Solomon Islands	Zambia
Burundi	Ethiopia	Laos	Nepal	Somalia	**Zimbabwe**
Cambodia	Gambia	Lesotho	Nicaragua	Sudan	
Cameroon	Georgia	Liberia	Niger	Tajikistan	

Lower-middle-income economies (54)—GNP per capita US$756 to US$2,995

Albania	**Colombia**	Guatemala	Lithuania	**Peru**	**Thailand**
Algeria	Cuba	Guyana	Macedonia	**Philippines**	Tonga
Belarus	Djibouti	Honduras	Maldives	Romania	Tunisia
Belize	Dominican	Iran	Marshall Islands	**Russia**	Turkmenistan
Bolivia	Republic	Iraq	Micronesia	Samoa	Vanuatu
Bosnia &	Ecuador	Jamaica	**Morocco**	**Sri Lanka**	West Bank and
Herzegovina	**Egypt**	**Jordan**	Namibia	St. Vincent	Gaza
Bulgaria	El Salvador	Kazakhstan	Papua	Suriname	Yugoslavia
Cape Verde	Equatorial Guinea	Kiribati	New Guinea	Swaziland	
China	Fiji	Latvia	Paraguay	Syria	

Upper-middle-income economies (38)—GNP per capita US$2,996 to US$9,265

American Samoa	Chile	Grenada	Mayotte	**Saudi Arabia**	Trinidad & Tobago
Antigua &	Costa Rica	**Hungary**	**Mexico**	Seychelles	**Turkey**
Barbuda	Croatia	Isle of Man	**Oman**	**Slovakia**	Uruguay
Argentina	**Czech Republic**	Lebanon	Palau	**South Africa**	**Venezuela**
Bahrain	Dominica	Libya	Panama	**South Korea**	
Botswana	Estonia	**Malaysia**	**Poland**	St. Kitts & Nevis	
Brazil	Gabon	Mauritius	Puerto Rico	St. Lucia	

High-income economies (52)—GNP per capita US$9,266 or more

Andorra	Cayman Islands	Greenland	Liechtenstein	No. Mariana	Sweden
Aruba	Channel Islands	Guam	Luxembourg	Islands	Switzerland
Australia	Cyprus	Hong Kong,	Macao, China	Norway	United Arab
Austria	Denmark	China	Malta	Portugal	Emirates
Bahamas	Faeroe Islands	Iceland	Monaco	Qatar	United Kingdom
Barbados	Finland	Ireland	Netherlands	San Marino	United States
Belgium	France	**Israel**	New Caledonia	Singapore	Virgin Islands
Bermuda	Germany	Japan	New Zealand	Spain	(U.S.)
Canada	Greece	Kuwait			

Source: World Bank and S&P's Emerging Markets Data Base (EMDB).

Table 2.1. Economic Characteristics of S&P/IFC Emerging Market Countries

Country	Market Cap (US$ millions) 1998	GDP (US$ millions) 1999	Market Cap/GDP	GNP per Capita (US$) 1999
Argentina	45,332	283,166	0.16	7,550
Bahrain	6,770	6,600	1.03	7,640
Brazil	160,887	751,505	0.21	4,350
Chile	51,866	67,469	0.77	4,630
China	231,322	989,465	0.23	780
Colombia	13,357	86,605	0.15	2,170
Czech Republic	12,045	53,111	0.23	5,020
Egypt	24,381	89,148	0.27	1,380
Hungary	14,028	48,436	0.29	4,640
India	105,188	447,292	0.24	440
Indonesia	22,104	142,511	0.16	600
Israel	39,628	100,840	0.39	16,310
Jordan	5,838	8,073	0.72	1,630
Malaysia	98,557	79,039	1.25	3,390
Mexico	91,746	483,737	0.19	4,440
Morocco	15,676	34,998	0.45	1,190
Nigeria	2,887	35,045	0.08	260
Oman	4,392	19,600	0.22	4,940
Pakistan	5,418	58,154	0.09	470
Peru	11,645	51,933	0.22	2,130
Philippines	35,314	76,559	0.46	1,050
Poland	20,461	155,166	0.13	4,070
Russia	20,958	401,442	0.05	2,250
Slovakia	965	19,712	0.05	3,770
South Africa	170,252	131,127	1.30	3,170
South Korea	114,593	406,940	0.28	8,490
Sri Lanka	1,705	15,958	0.11	820
Thailand	34,903	124,369	0.28	2,010
Turkey	33,646	185,691	0.18	2,900
Venezuela	7,587	102,222	0.07	3,680
Zimbabwe	1,310	5,608	0.23	530
Saudi Arabia	42,563	139,383	0.31	6,900

Source: Based on data from S&P's EMBD.

Figure 2.1. GNP per Capita and Market Cap/GDP for Emerging versus Frontier Markets, 1999

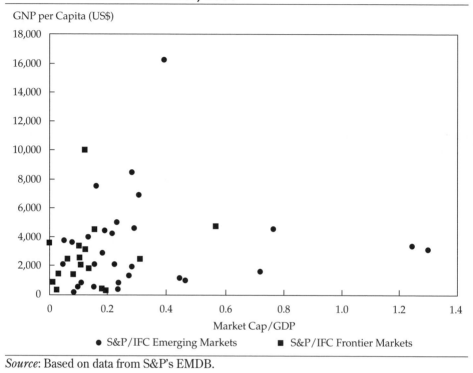

GNP per Capita (US$)

Market Cap/GDP

● S&P/IFC Emerging Markets   ■ S&P/IFC Frontier Markets

Source: Based on data from S&P's EMDB.

Overall, one observes that countries classified as "emerging" by S&P/IFC and MSCI EMF fall just below developed markets. The World Bank designates most of these emerging economies as upper-middle-income countries. In addition, even though the ratio of market cap to GDP for emerging market countries is less than that found in developed economies, it is still at the upper end of economies outside the developed world. Indeed, when the 113 less-developed countries are ranked on the ratio of market cap to GDP, the 32 defined as emerging in Table 2.1 have an average percentile rank of 80.3; the 20 frontier markets, 67.3; and the unclassified markets, 29.9.

Measures of Market and Company Size. For further insight into the relative openness and attractiveness of emerging markets for foreign portfolio investment, emerging market countries can also be compared with developed and frontier markets based on five characteristics related to size:
• relative market cap,
• number of companies listed in stock exchange,

Table 2.2. Economic Characteristics of Developed Market Countries

Country	Market Cap (US$ millions) 1998	GDP (US$ millions) 1999	Market Cap/GDP	GNP per Capita (US$) 1999
New Zealand	89,373	54,651	1.64	13,990
Singapore	94,469	84,945	1.11	24,150
Ireland	29,956	93,410	0.32	21,470
Portugal	62,954	113,716	0.55	11,030
Greece	79,992	125,088	0.64	12,110
Finland	154,518	129,661	1.19	24,730
Norway	56,285	152,943	0.37	33,470
Denmark	98,881	174,280	0.57	32,050
Austria	34,106	208,173	0.16	25,430
Sweden	278,707	238,682	1.17	26,750
Belgium	245,657	248,404	0.99	24,650
Switzerland	689,199	258,550	2.67	38,380
Netherlands	603,182	393,692	1.53	25,140
Australia	874,283	404,033	2.16	20,950
Spain	402,180	595,927	0.67	14,800
Canada	543,394	634,898	0.86	20,140
Italy	569,731	1,170,970	0.49	20,170
France	991,484	1,432,320	0.69	24,170
United Kingdom	2,374,273	1,441,790	1.65	23,590
Germany	1,093,962	2,111,940	0.52	25,620
Japan	2,495,757	4,346,920	0.57	32,030
United States	13,451,352	9,152,100	1.47	31,910

- average company market cap for the market,
- number of actively traded stocks, and
- number of stocks open to foreign investors.

▣ *Relative market cap.* **Table 2.3** reports the average market cap, ratio of market cap to GNP, and GNP per capita for each market classification. Market cap is highly correlated with the classification of a market. Relative to the frontier or "other" markets, the emerging markets have the highest average market cap. The result is similar for the data in **Figure 2.3**. The data in Table 2.1 exhibit the same pattern—very clear distinctions in terms of market cap between each of the classifications. **Figure 2.4** shows market cap for S&P/IFC emerging markets and developed markets as of July 2001. The top nine market caps belong to developed markets. After these nine markets, no clear distinction seems to exist between emerging and developed markets. In contrast, a clear distinction is apparent between frontier and emerging markets.

Figure 2.2. GNP per Capita and Market Cap/GDP for Emerging versus Developed Markets, 1999

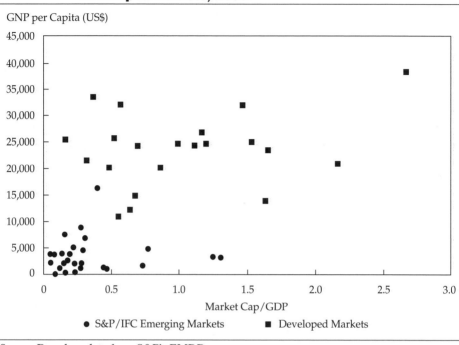

Source: Based on data from S&P's EMDB.

■ *Number of companies listed in stock exchange.* Another measure of the relative size of a financial market is the number of companies listed for trading on it. **Figure 2.5** shows the ranking of emerging and developed markets by the number of listed firms for July 2001. Surprisingly, except for the extremely large developed markets, such as the United States, Japan, and the United Kingdom, there does not seem to be much difference between the number of

Table 2.3. Characteristics of Emerging and Frontier Capital Markets, as of 1999

Markets	No. of Companies	Market Cap (US$ millions)	Market Cap/ GNP	GNP per Capita (US$)
Emerging	32	45,228	0.34	3,556
Frontier	19	1,573	0.16	2,676
Other	19	1,267	0.07	1,540

Source: Based on data from S&P's EMDB.

Figure 2.3. Emerging Markets Ranked by Market Capitalization, 1998

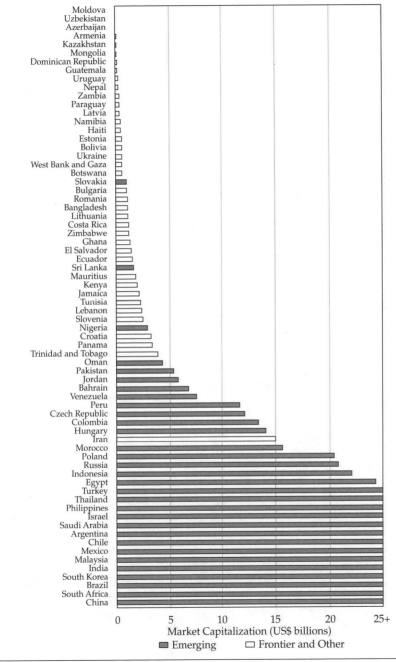

Source: Based on data from S&P's EMDB.

Figure 2.4. Developed and Emerging Markets Ranked by Market Capitalization, July 2001

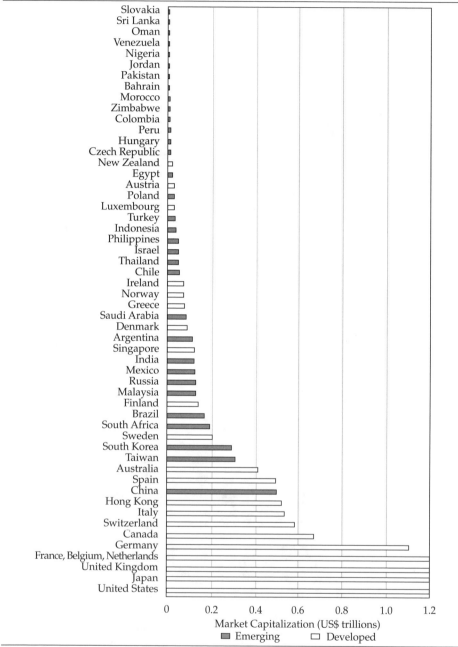

Market Capitalization (US$ trillions)

■ Emerging   □ Developed

Note: United States: US$13.15 trillion; Japan: US$2.63 trillion; United Kingdom: US$2.14 trillion; France: US$1.89 trillion.

Source: Based on data from S&P's EMDB.

Figure 2.5. Number of Publicly Listed Companies in Emerging and Developed Markets, July 2001

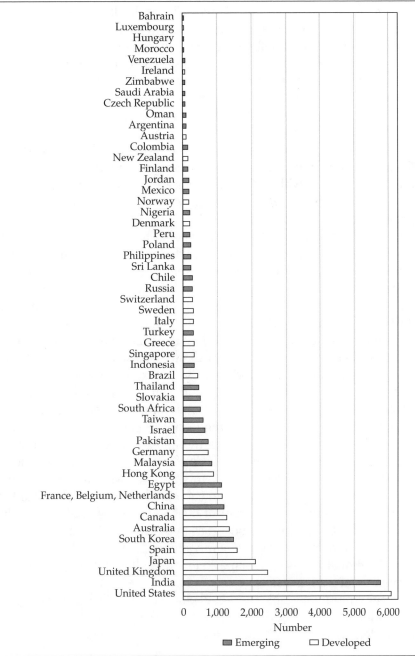

Source: Based on data from S&P's EMDB.

listed firms in the two sets of markets. So, emerging markets are smaller in market cap than developed markets but do have a similar number of listed firms.

■ *Average company market cap.* By combining the data in Figures 2.4 and 2.5, one can calculate the average company market cap in each market. Not surprisingly, given the results shown in the prior figures, **Figure 2.6** shows a significant difference in the size of the market cap of the average company in developed and emerging markets. When ranked according to average company size, 15 out of the top 20 markets were developed markets.

Hence, emerging markets differ not only in size of the market as a whole but also in average company size. In other words, simply having a large number of companies does not make a market attractive. This view is reinforced if one considers how many of the listed stocks are actively traded within the domestic market and which of these stocks are open to foreign investment.

■ *Number of actively traded stocks.* One way to assess the level of trading activity and openness is to consider how S&P constructs two of its most popular S&P/IFC emerging market indexes—the Global Index (or S&P/IFCG) and the Investable Index (S&P/IFCI). The Global Index includes the most actively traded stocks in a market, which can represent as much as 60–75 percent of the total cap of all listed stocks in each emerging market country. **Table 2.4** shows the number of listed companies and the market cap included in the S&P/IFCG Index. In this table, actively traded companies account for a relatively small percentage of the total. For example, India had the second largest number of listed companies, with about 5,900 stocks, yet had only 130 listed companies included in the S&P/IFCG Index. Other markets, such as Egypt, South Korea, Pakistan, Slovakia, and South Africa, also had a large number of listed companies but only a small number of them actively traded enough to be included. In fact, on average, only 18 percent of companies are actively traded enough to be included in the index. (Note, however, that the proportion ranges from a high of 38 percent for Morocco to a low of about 2 percent for India.) The companies in the S&P/IFCG Index represent a significant portion of the capitalization in each market. In general, a country's S&P/IFCG stocks do meet the target of 60–75 percent of total market cap, although significant deviations do occur, as in the case of Argentina.

■ *Number of stocks open to foreign investment.* The Investable Index tries to capture the global exposure of a market by including only stocks that
• are open to foreign investors,
• have a minimum investable market capitalization of US$50 million,
• have traded at least US$20 million over the past year, and
• have traded on at least half the local exchange trading days.

Figure 2.6. Average Company Market Capitalization, July 2001

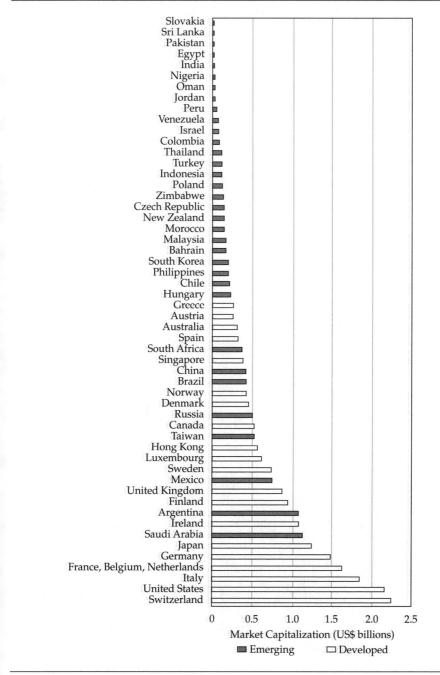

Market Capitalization (US$ billions)

■ Emerging   □ Developed

Source: Based on data from S&P's EMDB.

Table 2.4. Characteristics of All Listed Shares and Companies Included in S&P/IFC Global Index, as of July 2001

	All Listed Shares		Global Index Shares			
Country	No. of Companies	Market Cap (US$ millions)	No. of Companies	Percent of All Listed Companies	Market Cap (US$ millions)	Percent of Total Market Cap
Argentina	115	128,539	23	20.0	7,480	5.8
Bahrain	41	6,103	13	31.7	4,240	69.5
Brazil	435	142,848	82	18.9	85,505	59.9
Chile	255	50,503	42	16.5	33,341	66.0
China	1,151	553,733	246	21.4	217,771	39.3
Colombia	126	9,954	18	14.3	4,328	43.5
Czech Republic	118	7,967	18	15.3	5,339	67.0
Egypt	1,083	26,041	70	6.5	6,990	26.8
Greece	338	72,530	64	18.9	41,515	57.2
Hungary	57	8,531	16	28.1	7,479	87.7
India	5,939	95,353	130	2.2	61,869	64.9
Indonesia	308	24,876	66	21.4	16,898	67.9
Israel	647	48,041	47	7.3	31,093	64.7
Jordan	163	5,683	33	20.2	3,985	70.1
Malaysia	809	106,250	134	16.6	71,884	67.7
Mexico	169	113,125	57	33.7	82,445	72.9
Morocco	55	9,172	21	38.2	7,472	81.5
Nigeria	194	5,392	27	13.9	3,758	69.7
Oman	92	3,210	29	31.5	1,914	59.6
Pakistan	757	4,448	42	5.5	2,580	58.0
Peru	208	10,587	26	12.5	5,707	53.9
Philippines	231	40,087	59	25.5	15,426	38.5
Poland	231	20,454	34	14.7	14,776	72.2
Russia	247	50,203	17	6.9	35,737	71.2
Saudi Arabia	76	69,617	21	27.6	49,831	71.6
Slovakia	850	887	10	1.2	622	70.1
South Africa	566	153,147	66	11.7	72,281	47.2
South Korea	1,352	159,681	159	11.8	116,800	73.1
Sri Lanka	237	892	50	21.1	531	59.5
Taiwan	587	188,443	117	19.9	119,681	63.5
Thailand	441	30,265	62	14.1	20,461	67.6
Turkey	310	24,797	58	18.7	19,865	80.1
Venezuela	62	7,112	14	22.6	3,318	46.7
Zimbabwe	74	8,392	22	29.7	3,064	36.5

Source: Based on data from S&P's EMDB.

Exhibit 2.2 provides a summary of "openness" to foreign investors by country. Note that of the 33 markets listed in Table 1.1, only 18 of them are 100 percent open to foreign investment. The remaining 15 markets are either closed to foreign investment or have varying restrictions. The most common restrictions include:

- special classes of shares for foreign owners;
- sector ownership restrictions, such as banking or broadcast media;[6]
- limits on ownership held by a single foreign shareholder;
- company ownership limits that differ from national law; and,
- national limits on aggregate foreign ownership.

For most of the markets classified as "open," a very high proportion of the companies in the Global Index pass the tests for inclusion in the S&P/IFCI Index. We find a much smaller proportion of companies passing the tests for inclusion in the S&P/IFCI when the markets are less than 100 percent open. For example, Jordan and Zimbabwe had less than one-third of the companies in the S&P/IFCI. Of course, the differences are much more stark when the markets are cited as closed and there are no companies in the S&P/IFCI. For example, Bahrain is closed to foreign investment. The openness of a market to foreign investment is clearly an important issue for investors.

Market Liquidity

Liquidity varies for all markets, but the tendency toward *illiquidity* in emerging markets is one of the primary factors that differentiate them from developed countries. Thus, a major consideration for investors in emerging markets is the liquidity of their financial positions, or the ability to get in and out of investments quickly and at low cost. In contrast, developed markets offer much greater depth of trading (that is, the ability to make a large trade without an accompanying large change in the traded stock's price). It is possible to gain a sense of this capacity within a particular market through the use of turnover ratios.

Turnover ratios are calculated as the ratio of value traded over one month to the total market cap. A high turnover ratio means that a large number of the shares outstanding were traded. One would expect high turnover ratios to be associated with greater levels of liquidity; thus, the larger, more developed markets should exhibit higher turnover ratios. **Figure 2.7** shows the distribution of turnover ratios for a number of developed and emerging markets. With a few exceptions, notably South Korea, Taiwan, and Turkey,

---

[6]Restrictions on foreign ownership of print and/or broadcast media are not uncommon in developed markets.

Exhibit 2.2. Market Openness to Foreign Investments

Country	Summary of Market Openness to Foreign Investments
Argentina	Considered 100 percent open. Some corporate limitations apply.
Bahrain	Closed to foreign investment.
Brazil	Considered generally open. Since May 1991, foreign institutions may own up to 49 percent of voting common stock and 100 percent of nonvoting participating preferred stock. Some corporate limitations apply (e.g., Petrobras common stock is off limits, and voting-class stock of banks is not available).
Chile	Considered 100 percent open.
China	Foreign institutions may purchase B-class shares listed on Chinese stock exchanges, H-class shares listed on the Hong Kong Stock Exchange, and other classes of shares offered and listed in the United States and United Kingdom without restriction.
Colombia	Considered generally open since 1 February 1991.
Czech Republic	Considered 100 percent open, except for banks.
Egypt	No restrictions precluding foreign participation in the market and no rules against repatriation of profits. In a few exceptions to this rule, certain companies' charters do not permit foreign shareholders.
Greece	Considered 100 percent open.
Hungary	Considered 100 percent open.
India	Considered open since 1 November 1992. Foreign investment institutions (FIIs) can register for primary and secondary markets. Investments are subject to a ceiling of 24 percent of a company's issued share capital for the aggregate holdings of all FIIs and to 5 percent for the holding of any single FII.
Indonesia	Since 1989, foreigners may hold up to 49 percent of all companies, except banks. The Bank Act of 1992 allowed foreigners to hold up to 49 percent of the listed shares in three categories of banks—private national, state owned, and foreign joint venture.
Israel	In general, 100 percent open to foreign investment.
Jordan	Considered generally open up to 49 percent of listed companies' capital.
Malaysia	With the exception of bank and finance company stocks, most stocks are generally 100 percent available to foreign investors.
Mexico	Considered generally 100 percent open, except for banks and other financial institutions or groups, for which foreign ownership is limited to 30 percent of total capital (although certain classes may be freely available to foreign investors).
Nigeria	Although the Nigerian stock market is technically open to foreign portfolio investment, the secondary market is virtually nonexistent.
Oman	Closed.
Pakistan	Considered 100 percent open since 22 February 1991.
Peru	Generally considered 100 percent open.
Philippines	National law requires that Philippine nationals own a minimum of 60 percent of the shares issued by domestic firms. To ensure compliance, Philippine companies typically issue two classes of stock—A-shares, which may be held only by Philippine nationals, and B-shares, which both foreign and Philippine investors may buy. Media, retail trade, and rural banking companies are closed to foreign investors.
Poland	The market is considered 100 percent open.
Russia	In general, 100 percent open to foreign investment. Banks need central bank approval.
Saudi Arabia	Closed to foreign investment.

Exhibit 2.2. Market Openness to Foreign Investments (continued)

Country	Summary of Market Openness to Foreign Investments
Slovakia	In general, 100 percent open to foreign investment. Banks need central bank approval.
South Africa	The market is generally considered 100 percent open, although some corporate limitations may apply regarding shares issued in privatizations.
South Korea	The Korean authorities have committed to gradually opening their stock and capital markets to foreign investors since they were first opened to foreign investment on 1 January 1992. At that time, regulations took effect allowing authorized foreign investors to acquire up to 10 percent of the capital of listed companies. Since then, the general foreign limit has been increased several times, to 12 percent in January 1995, 15 percent in July 1995, 18 percent in April 1996, and most recently, to 20 percent on 1 October 1996. In addition to the general limits, some lower corporate limits apply for certain firms. Under regulations in effect since July 1992, companies with existing foreign shareholdings can apply to the Korea Securities and Exchange Commission to increase the limit to 25 percent. The ceiling in such cases would automatically decline if foreign-held shares were sold to domestic investors.
Sri Lanka	The market is considered 100 percent open, except for banks, which are 49 percent open. Some companies limit foreign investment.
Taiwan	Authorities permit foreign institutions meeting fairly strict registration requirements to invest in listed stocks, up to a 30 percent limit of aggregate foreign investment in a company's issued capital.
Thailand	Thai laws restrict foreign shareholdings in Thai companies engaged in certain areas of business. The Banking Law restricts foreign ownership in banks to 25 percent. The Alien Business Law, administered by the Ministry of Commerce, restricts foreign ownership of stocks in specified sectors to 49 percent. In addition, other laws provide for similar restrictions. Company bylaws impose restrictions that range from 15 percent to 65 percent.
Turkey	The market is considered 100 percent open since August 1989.
Venezuela	Stocks are generally considered 100 percent open.
Zimbabwe	The Zimbabwe Stock Exchange was effectively closed to foreign investment by virtue of severe exchange controls until new regulations were introduced in June 1993. The new regulations on foreign investment permitted foreigners to purchase up to 25 percent of the shares outstanding of listed companies. The limit was raised to 35 percent by the Reserve Bank of Zimbabwe on 1 January 1996, and then again to 40 percent.

Source: Standard & Poors (2000)

almost all of the emerging markets have turnover ratios lower than 5 percent, well below those found in more developed ones. Interestingly, a turnover ratio of 5 percent seems to be the threshold that separates developed markets from emerging markets. For example, whereas a developed market such as the New York Stock Exchange (NYSE) trades almost 8–9 percent of its market value during a typical month, Mexico trades 2 percent of its total market cap and Peru trades less than 1 percent in a similar period of time.

Figure 2.7.   Average Turnover Ratio for Emerging and Developed Markets, 2002

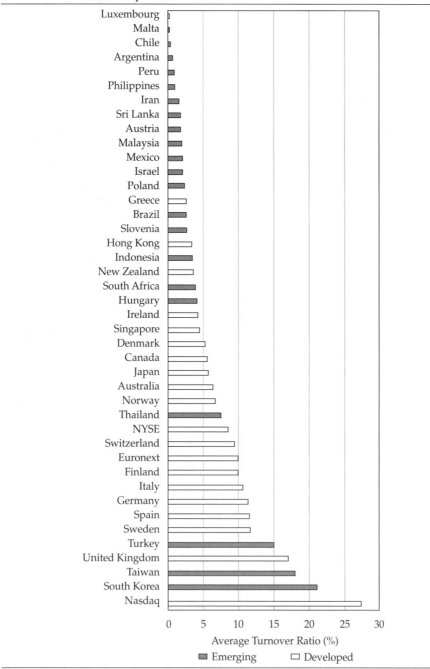

Source: Based on data from World Federation of Exchanges.

©2003, The Research Foundation of AIMR™

Examining the turnover ratio in dollar terms is also useful because this metric gives some indication of relative volume of money moving in and out of a market in a year. **Figure 2.8** compares the average daily U.S. dollar value of shares traded during 2002 in developed and emerging markets. For example, the average daily dollar value of shares traded on the NYSE exceeded US$10 trillion, and the average daily value traded on the Tokyo exchange exceeded US$1.5 trillion. In contrast, Mexico traded a daily total of US$32 billion in shares, and Indonesia, a total of US$13 billion. In light of the magnitude of transactions that typical major institutional investors conduct each day, the levels of trading in Mexico and Indonesia are low. As a means of emphasizing this point, consider that a standard trade for such an institutional investor may be 10,000 shares at US$40 a share (for a trade value of US$400,000). On the NYSE, the US$10 trillion in total trading represents more than 25 million trades of US$400,000 each day. The Indonesian market's average daily rate of US$13 billion represents only 32,500 daily trades of US$400,000. Turnover data from 2002 for the set of developed and emerging markets portrayed in Figure 2.8 highlight this vast difference in the magnitude of trading volume. Indeed, except for Taiwan and South Korea, most emerging market trading volumes pale in comparison with those of developed markets.

Transparency, Competitiveness, and Corruption

Three other characteristics often cited as risk factors in emerging markets—transparency, competitiveness, and corruption—are important because they determine the ability for investors to gain information and develop performance expectations. Every market poses challenges in these areas, but the difficulties are magnified in emerging markets.

Transparency. PricewaterhouseCoopers has designed an index to measure transparency according to five dimensions for 35 countries. This Opacity Index, also known as the "O-Factor," is constructed based on data from interviews with CFOs, bankers, equity analysts, and PricewaterhouseCoopers employees. The five dimensions are corruption, legal, economics, accounting, and regulatory. The O-Factor itself is the simple average of the index values for each dimension.

The index is useful because the cost of doing business in countries with greater opacity is higher and external investment capital is more difficult to obtain. **Table 2.5** shows the index values for each dimension and the O-Factor for the countries it covers for the year 2001. Two surprises on the list are the high ranking of Chile, an emerging market, and the low ranking of Japan, a major developed market. Chile scores well on low corruption and on transparent legal and accounting systems. On the other hand, Japan scores relatively

Figure 2.8. Average Daily Value of Shares Traded in Emerging and Developed Markets, 2002

Note: NYSE: US$10,311 billion; Nasdaq: US$7,254 billion.

Table 2.5. PricewaterhouseCoopers Opacity Index, 2001

Country	Corruption	Legal	Economics	Accounting	Regulatory	O-Factor
Singapore	13	32	42	38	23	29
Chile	30	32	52	28	36	36
United States	25	37	42	25	48	36
United Kingdom	15	40	53	45	38	38
Hong Kong	25	55	49	53	42	45
Italy	28	57	73	26	56	48
Mexico	42	58	57	29	52	48
Hungary	37	48	53	65	47	50
Israel	18	61	70	62	51	53
Uruguay	44	56	61	56	49	53
Greece	49	51	76	49	62	57
Egypt	33	52	73	68	64	58
Lithuania	46	50	71	59	66	58
Peru	46	58	65	61	57	58
Colombia	48	66	77	55	55	60
Japan	22	72	72	81	53	60
South Africa	45	53	68	82	50	60
Argentina	56	63	68	49	67	61
Brazil	53	59	68	63	62	61
Taiwan	45	70	71	56	61	61
Pakistan	48	66	81	62	54	62
Venezuela	53	68	80	50	67	63
India	55	68	59	79	58	64
Poland	56	61	77	55	72	64
Guatemala	59	49	80	71	66	65
Thailand	55	65	70	78	66	67
Ecuador	60	72	78	68	62	68
Kenya	60	72	78	72	63	69
Czech Republic	57	97	62	77	62	71
Romania	61	68	77	78	73	71
South Korea	48	79	76	90	73	73
Turkey	51	72	87	80	81	74
Indonesia	70	86	82	68	69	75
Russia	78	84	90	81	84	84
China	62	100	87	86	100	87

Source: Based on data from PricewaterhouseCoopers.

poorly on transparency in its legal and accounting systems. Overall, however, Table 2.5 shows that countries that score high on one factor tend to score high on the others. This phenomenon is confirmed in **Table 2.6**, which shows the correlation between the different factors. All of the correlations are very high, indicating the general tendency for markets to score consistently across different factors.

Table 2.6. Correlation of Factors in the 2001 Opacity Index

	Corruption	Legal	Economics	Accounting	Regulatory
Corruption	1.000				
Legal	0.666	1.000			
Economics	0.692	0.662	1.000		
Accounting	0.532	0.666	0.566	1.000	
Regulatory	0.773	0.747	0.822	0.596	1.000

Competitiveness. The International Institute for Management Development (IMD) World Competitiveness Index is a widely used overall measure of the relative competitiveness of a particular country. Topping the list for 2002 was the United States. The highest emerging market on the list was Chile, ranked 20th.

Corruption. Finally, Transparency International provides an annual corruption perception index (CPI) that ranks 100 countries on the relative influence of corruption, as shown in **Figure 2.9** for a representative set of developed and emerging markets. Each country is scored on a scale of 1 through 10, with 10 representing the least amount of corruption.

Once again, the distinction between developed and emerging markets is dramatic. Although a few markets, such as Chile and Israel, rank high on the list and a few developed markets score lower, developed markets are generally perceived to have relatively less corruption than emerging markets.

The CPI is calculated from a composite of a number of different sources, including the PricewaterhouseCoopers' O-Factor and IMD's competitiveness ranking. **Table 2.7** shows the IMD ranking, the CPI ranking, and the O-Factor for the 50 countries covered by the IMD competitiveness survey. (Note that not all countries had an O-Factor available.) The correlations among the three measures are high enough for one measure to be a proxy for the others. Not surprisingly, the correlation between the IMD and CPI index rankings is 0.88. In other words, the indexes basically report the same thing.

Figure 2.9. Corruption Perception Index for 2001

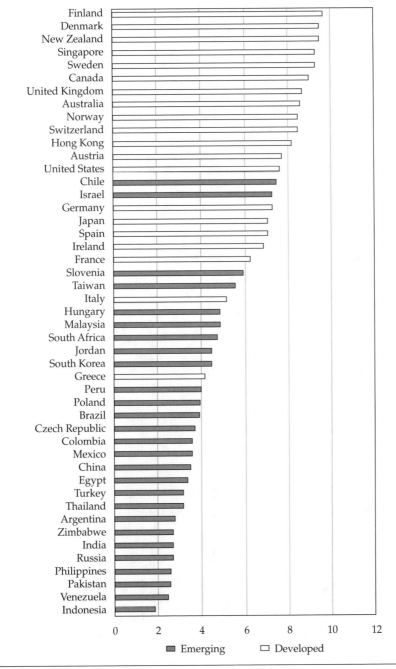

Source: Based on data from Transparency International.

Table 2.7. IMD, CPI, and O-Factor 2001 Rankings

Country	IMD	CPI	O-Factor
United States	100.00	77	36
Finland	84.35	97	
Luxembourg	84.30	90	
Netherlands	82.80	90	
Singapore	81.20	93	
Denmark	80.40	95	
Switzerland	79.50	95	
Canada	79.01	90	
Hong Kong	77.80	82	45
Ireland	76.20	69	
Sweden	76.19	93	
Iceland	74.70	94	
Austria	74.60	78	
Australia	74.10	86	
Germany	70.90	73	
United Kingdom	69.90	87	
Norway	67.70	85	
Belgium	66.70	71	
New Zealand	66.50	95	
Chile	65.60	75	36
Estonia	63.40	56	
France	61.60	63	
Spain	61.50	71	
Taiwan	61.30	56	61
Israel	60.50	73	53
Malaysia	59.70	49	
Hungary	56.70	49	50
Czech Republic	55.30	37	71
Japan	54.30	71	60
China	52.20	35	87
Italy	51.80	52	48
Portugal	49.30	63	
Thailand	47.90	32	
Brazil	47.60	40	61
Greece	46.90	42	57
Slovakia	45.70	37	
Slovenia	45.50	60	
South Africa	43.90	48	60
South Korea	56.80	45	73
Philippines	41.50	26	
Mexico	41.39	36	48
India	40.70	27	64
Russia	39.00	27	84
Colombia	37.10	36	60
Poland	30.20	40	64
Turkey	27.90	32	74
Indonesia	26.86	19	75
Argentina	26.00	28	61
Venezuela	25.85	25	63

Note: The CPI scale has been rescaled from a basis of 10 to 100.

Probit Analysis

Probit analysis can assess the probability of a country being classified as an emerging market [i.e., Prob(EM)] based on certain variables or attributes. This analysis is useful in determining whether the variables used in the probit do explain the classification of a market as emerging. In the example below, the variables that seem to be the most relevant (according to the analysis in this chapter) are used—market cap, GNP per capita, and the ratio of investable capitalization to GDP.[7] So,

$$\text{Prob(EM)} = \alpha_0 + \alpha_1 \times \text{Market cap} + \alpha_2 \times \text{Ratio} + \alpha_3 \times \text{GNP per capita}.$$

In the following example, the numbers under each of the coefficients are the maximum likelihood estimates of the coefficients, and the numbers in parentheses are Chi-square statistics.

Prob(EM) =	α_0	+	$\alpha_1 \times$ Market cap	+	$\alpha_2 \times$ Ratio	+	$\alpha_3 \times$ GNP per capita
	−1.29		0.0002		6.81		−0.00
	(12.1)		(14.8)		(1.57)		(0.15)

The coefficients on market cap and ratio are positive, and the one for market cap is significant at the 1 percent level. **Figure 2.10** shows the probability[8] of a particular country being classified as an emerging market based on market cap, ratio of market cap to GDP, and GDP per capita.

As reflected in Figure 2.10, these variables discriminate well among emerging markets and less-developed markets, although some cases suggest that our model does not explain completely what makes an emerging market. These exceptions, however, are few. For example, a few markets classified as frontier markets and other—Iran, Trinidad and Tobago, Panama, Mauritius, and Jamaica—appear to have higher probabilities of being classified as emerging markets. Among the emerging market countries, the Slovak Republic, Sri Lanka, and Nigeria have low probabilities of receiving this classification. Despite the exceptions, the three variables are good indicators of emerging market status. (And one would not be surprised if the anomaly markets were reclassified soon.)

In summary, probit analysis suggests that, relative to the other 150 less-developed markets, those classified as emerging markets tend to have higher income levels, a higher ratio of market cap to GDP, and greater market cap. Moreover, market cap seems to be the most important determinant.

---

[7]In our analysis, the dependent variable takes the value of 1 if a country is classified as an emerging market by S&P/IFC and a value of 0 otherwise.

[8]Probabilities are determined by using the probit analysis coefficient estimates to determine a z-score for each country and then using a cumulative normal distribution to determine the probability.

Figure 2.10. Probit Analysis for Various Emerging and Other Less-Developed Markets

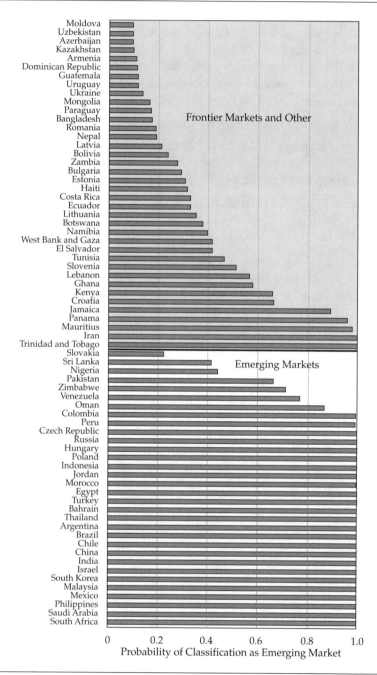

Identifying Emerging Markets

The markets identified as emerging by either S&P/IFC or MSCI EMF in Table 1.1 vary greatly in market size, available information, and governance. In general, however, these countries tend to rank just below developed markets in many of the characteristics examined in this chapter, such as liquidity, corruption, and size. To highlight the relative position among emerging financial markets, **Table 2.8** compares a representative set of emerging markets with Greece, which recently graduated from the "emerging" class and was reclassified as "developed." To create this table, a score of 1 was awarded for each dimension in which the sample country ranks higher (closer to the developed nations) than Greece. For example, markets such as South Korea and Taiwan rank higher than Greece on all dimensions except relative GDP. Other markets ranking just below South Korea and Taiwan are Brazil and South Africa.

From Table 2.8, two general groups of emerging markets can be identified. Group 1 contains Brazil, Mexico, South Korea, South Africa, and Taiwan. Group 2 contains all the other countries in Table 2.8. The difference between the two groups is the availability of information. Markets that are larger, liquid, and more transparent and suffer from less corruption tend to have better information flows and consequently tend to be more efficient. Although this categorization is somewhat artificial, it does help demonstrate the interrelationship among the characteristics that allow a market to be considered developed. Even though emerging markets share common characteristics, significant disparities exist among them.

Table 2.8. Ranking of Various Emerging Markets Relative to Greece
(value = 1 if rank is higher than Greece)

Country	GDP	Size Total	Size Investable	Liquidity Turnover (%)	Liquidity Turnover ($)	Corruption CPI	Total Score
Argentina		1					1
Bahrain							0
Brazil		1	1	1	1		4
Chile						1	1
China		1	1				2
Colombia							0
Czech Republic							0
Egypt							0
Greece	1	1	1	1	1	1	6
Hungary				1		1	2
India		1	1				2
Indonesia				1			1
Israel	1					1	2
Jordan						1	1
Malaysia		1				1	2
Mexico		1	1		1		3
Morocco							0
Nigeria							0
Oman							0
Pakistan							0
Peru							0
Philippines							0
Poland							0
Russia		1					1
Saudi Arabia		1					1
Slovakia				1		1	2
South Africa		1	1	1	1		4
South Korea		1	1	1	1	1	5
Sri Lanka							0
Taiwan		1	1	1	1	1	5
Thailand				1	1		2
Turkey				1	1		2
Venezuela							0
Zimbabwe							0

3. Diversification, Return, and Volatility

Despite the risk factors outlined in Chapter 2, two main characteristics of emerging markets should be attractive for portfolio managers—their low correlation with world equity markets and their potential future growth in market cap. Investors, however, must also carefully evaluate volatility in these markets.

The low correlation between emerging and global markets implies that adding a portfolio of emerging markets securities to a diversified developed markets portfolio would result in a reduction of six percentage points in the total portfolio's volatility while keeping the expected return unchanged, according to Harvey (1995). With respect to potential growth in market cap, in 1992, emerging countries represented only 9 percent of the world's equity market cap but their GDP accounted for 19 percent of world GDP. At the end of 2002, emerging markets' share of the world market cap, as measured by S&P/IFC, had grown to 10.5 percent and their share of world GDP had increased to 20 percent, suggesting that great potential growth in market cap remains. In addition to finding low correlations between emerging and developed markets, Harvey found that listed companies operating in emerging markets tended to have higher average returns and higher volatility than those operating in developed markets.

The performance characteristics of emerging markets may have changed as a consequence of recent crises in emerging markets and the increased economic and financial integration of emerging markets into the global market. **Table 3.1** shows summary statistics of monthly returns for the 31 IFCI country indexes from January 1990 to January 2003. Twelve emerging markets registered negative geometric average returns. An investor who had followed a buy-and-hold strategy for each of the IFCI country portfolios (starting January 1990) would have lost money on 12 country portfolios by January 2003.

The recent lackluster performance of emerging markets is attributable to the series of financial crises that started with the Mexican "tequila" crisis in January 1995. Thereafter, the return on the S&P/IFCI Composite Index was negative and volatility increased. In contrast, between January 1990 and December 1994, average returns in emerging markets were substantially higher than those observed for the MSCI World Index and S&P 500 Index, albeit with higher volatility as well.

Table 3.1. Annualized Average Monthly Return for the S&P/IFCI Composite Index versus MSCI World and S&P 500 Indexes, January 1990–January 2003

Country	Arithmetic Annual Return	Geometric Annual Return	Annual Volatility of Return	Skewness	Excess Kurtosis
Argentina	16.8%	3.3%	50.7%	1.46	11.15
Brazil	27.2	8.5	61.6	0.68	4.54
Chile	15.5	12.8	26.4	0.05	0.83
China	0.6	−8.0	42.7	0.54	1.03
Colombia	15.7	9.6	37.6	0.99	1.88
Czech Republic	3.7	−2.9	37.9	1.62	10.12
Egypt	−17.2	−17.8	24.4	0.81	1.02
Greece	15.8	9.1	39.4	1.49	5.33
Hungary	20.0	12.2	42.5	1.14	5.84
India	2.5	−1.6	28.9	0.25	−0.11
Indonesia	0.1	−11.8	50.3	0.44	2.03
Israel	7.4	3.8	26.8	−0.47	−0.25
Jordan	10.5	9.8	14.3	0.59	1.13
Malaysia	6.5	−0.2	37.5	0.86	4.77
Mexico	15.3	9.6	34.2	−0.71	1.34
Morocco	2.6	1.2	17.1	0.45	0.16
Pakistan	11.9	2.3	44.3	0.37	1.25
Peru	12.7	8.8	29.3	0.28	2.69
Philippines	−2.2	−8.9	38.2	0.54	1.98
Poland	30.7	17.9	57.3	1.99	10.45
Portugal	12.1	9.8	23.3	0.40	0.89
Russia	27.4	1.2	71.1	0.10	1.48
Slovakia	−14.8	−17.1	27.6	0.07	−0.44
South Africa	13.0	9.2	28.5	−0.52	2.23
South Korea	8.8	−1.5	47.5	1.34	5.45
Sri Lanka	2.0	−4.8	37.9	0.79	3.94
Taiwan	7.3	0.8	37.3	1.21	3.02
Thailand	1.4	−7.6	43.7	0.44	1.20
Turkey	17.0	−2.7	63.6	0.75	1.33
Venezuela	33.8	18.7	58.4	0.51	1.94
Zimbabwe	29.3	20.0	46.3	−0.23	1.56
IFCI Composite	6.6	1.6	23.3	−0.61	1.68
MSCI World	3.4	2.3	15.1	−0.40	0.22
S&P 500	7.9	7.0	15.2	−0.44	0.43
January 1990–December 1994					
IFCI Composite	18.2	17.9	21.0	−0.02	0.40
MSCI World	2.8	1.7	14.8	−0.07	0.28
S&P 500	6.0	5.4	12.1	0.12	1.26
January 1994–January 2003					
IFCI Composite	−0.5	−1.9	24.5	−0.77	1.83
MSCI World	3.8	2.9	15.3	−0.60	0.28
S&P 500	9.1	7.8	16.7	−0.60	0.11

Source: Based on data from S&P's Emerging Markets Data Base (EMDB) and Datastream.

Bekaert and Harvey (1997) argued that four main factors contribute to higher volatility in emerging markets: asset concentration, stock market development and economic integration, market microstructure, and macroeconomic influences and political risk:

- *Asset concentration* refers to the degree of diversification and concentration that is intrinsic in the indexes for the different countries because the stocks represented in those indexes might not fully represent the actual diversification of the countries' industry mix.

- *Stock market development and economic integration* should decrease volatility because of the transition from local to international risk factors and because of the increased diversification of industries within the economy.

- *Market microstructure* refers to market liquidity and to information asymmetries between traders: As asymmetries decrease and liquidity increases, volatility should decrease.

- *Macroeconomic influences and political risk* negatively influence the volatility of the stock market, an effect represented by political and macroeconomic risks included in country risk ratings.

In addition to volatility, investors should also consider the changing correlation between emerging markets and global markets. After the Asian crisis in August 1997 and the Russian default in 1998, correlation increased between the S&P/IFCI Composite Index and both the S&P 500 and MSCI World indexes. The correlations have remained well above precrises levels, as shown in **Figure 3.1** and **Figure 3.2**.

Financial contagion, as observed during the Asian financial crisis, appears to be an important factor in increasing volatility in emerging markets and their correlation with developed markets. In general, contagion in equity markets is the spread of financial market turmoil from one country to the next, causing financial markets to move downward in a synchronized fashion. Factors that can augment the risk of contagion include weak economic fundamentals, macroeconomic similarities with other crisis countries, heavy exposure to certain financial agents, and the overall state of international financial markets.

Understanding the causes of financial contagion, however, is extremely difficult. Whether a purported instance of contagion actually occurred can be a much debated subject, largely because various technical definitions of contagion exist. Some economists argue that a shock in one country that is transmitted to another country constitutes contagion, independent of the previous correlation between those two markets. Others argue that it is necessary to identify exactly how shocks are propagated from one country to another: how much of the shock is propagated through trade, how much through investor

Figure 3.1. Correlation Coefficient between S&P 500 Monthly Total Return and S&P/IFCI Composite Monthly Total Return
(36-month moving average)

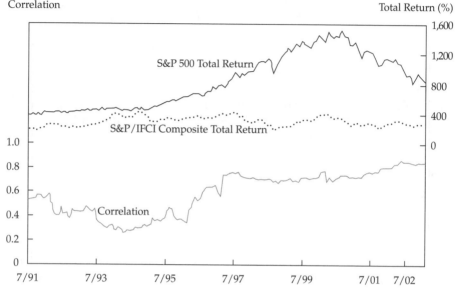

Note: Data from January 1990 to January 2003.
Source: Based on data from Bloomberg and S&P's EMDB.

behavior, and so on. They assert that, regardless of the magnitude, only the proportion of shock that is above and beyond that transmitted through "standard channels" (e.g., links via international trade) should be considered contagion. Forbes and Rigobon (2002) distinguished between the concepts of pure contagion (the idea that financial shocks are transmitted across markets and countries around the world) and "shift contagion." According to this view, the impact that a crisis in one market has on another country's market constitutes shift contagion only if the correlation between the two markets increases significantly during the crisis period.

Distinguishing between pure contagion and shift contagion can be useful for determining the effectiveness of international diversification in reducing portfolio risk during a crisis. The benefit of international diversification is significantly reduced if the correlation between different markets increases significantly during crises. Forbes and Rigobon also argued that the concept of shift contagion can be useful for multilateral organizations (e.g., the International Monetary Fund and World Bank). For example, if a certain country is affected by a crisis in another country as a result of shift contagion, financial

Figure 3.2. Moving Average for Correlation Coefficient between MSCI World Monthly Total Return and S&P/IFCI Composite Monthly Total Return
(36-month moving average)

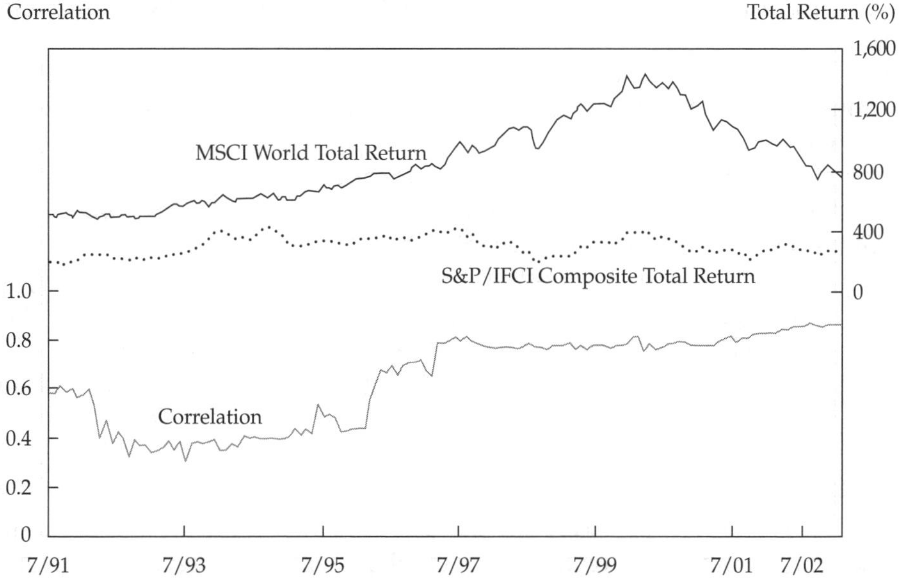

Note: Data from January 1990 to January 2003.
Source: Based on data from Bloomberg and S&P's EMDB.

assistance could help avoid extra contagion-induced volatility by providing stability to the financial markets. On the other hand, if a certain country was affected by a shock in another country with which it has strong economic ties (and high ongoing correlation), the effect would not constitute contagion. In this case, financial support from multilateral organizations would be suboptimal and would only delay any necessary market adjustments. Applying the definitions of pure and shift contagion, Forbes and Rigobon found little evidence to support the existence of shift contagion among the following crises they analyzed—the 1982 Mexican debt crisis, the 1992 exchange rate crises following the abandonment of the European Exchange Rate Mechanism, the 1994 Mexican tequila crisis, the 1997 Asian flu, the 1998 Russian cold, the 1999 Brazilian sneeze, and the 2000 Nasdaq rash.

Bekaert, Harvey, and Ng (2003) took a different approach from that of Forbes and Rigobon. Although they shared the definition of contagion as excess correlation, or greater correlation than what should be expected based on global, regional, and country-specific economic fundamentals, they applied an asset-pricing perspective to the study of contagion. They found no evidence of contagion during the Mexican crisis. But they demonstrated that correlation increased significantly during the Asian crisis, specifically within the Asian region. Even when increased correlation should have been expected because volatility increased, the magnitude of the increase was above normal levels during the Asian crisis. Furthermore, this increase was also substantial in countries that had little trade relationship with the initially affected countries and that had small fiscal deficits, very low external debt, and no major unemployment problems. Similarly, the Russian cold was indeed more virulent than the Asian flu, and its impact was immediately international. In contrast, the 1999 devaluation of the Brazilian real did not have external impact beyond countries with which Brazil had strong economic ties, which suggests that no contagion was associated with this event. Likewise, during the 2001 Argentine collapse, the market and currency crash had no effect on other emerging market countries (except probably Turkey, which had the same perceived potential problems as Argentina).

Summary

To the extent that an emerging market country is "emerging," it should experience a faster rate of capital accumulation and faster economic growth than a developed country. A diversified portfolio invested in such an emerging market country generally should outperform a portfolio of comparable industry composition invested in a developed country. In addition, Bekaert and Harvey (1997) show that volatility in an emerging market should decline and its correlation with developed markets should increase as the emerging market develops and becomes more transparent, efficient, and more integrated with developed markets and as the political and macroeconomic risks fall.

Actual performance of emerging markets between 1990 and 2002 was disappointing, as shown in Table 3.1. But there were exceptions. The IFCI Chile composite index recorded a geometric mean return of 12.8 percent a year, with a relatively low volatility of 26.4 percent a year. During the same period, the S&P 500 composite index had a geometric mean return of 7 percent and a volatility of 15.2 percent. The superior stock market performance in Chile was attributable to the combination of sustained high economic growth, macroeconomic stability, and liberalization of the financial market.

Investing in an emerging market thus is largely a bet on its emergence. Although the potential returns can be high and the benefits of diversification can be enticing, investors need to consider the high volatility and the impact of possible financial crises and contagion on their portfolios.

4. Efficiency in Emerging Markets

In efficient markets, security prices reflect all that is known about the assets underlying those securities. Thus, one's belief in the efficiency of a market has great significance for how one interprets observed prices. How much does the market know? The answer hinges on the quality of information available and how the market processes the information. Studies suggest that in developed markets, quality—of both information and processing—is reasonably good. This chapter explores whether the same conclusion holds for emerging markets. Specifically, we evaluate the availability of marketwide information and company-specific information and how such information is processed in emerging markets.

Market Information and the Risk-Free Rate

To address the difficulty of determining the availability of market information and the investment horizon, the term for which the local government is able to borrow at a fixed-interest rate—and thus the horizon for which investors are willing to commit—can be used as a proxy for the time span for which timely and reliable information is available. Hence, a market in which the government is able to borrow in the local currency at a fixed rate for 20 years suggests an overall faith in the institutions. Further, it suggests an environment in which the information is rich and reliable enough to attract investors to make such a commitment—an environment that should be closer to being efficient. In contrast, a market with only floating-rate debt indicates that investors are unwilling to commit to a fixed rate for long periods of time. Such conditions may be interpreted as evidence of a lack of reliable information.

Table 4.1 shows the longest-maturity fixed-rate local-currency-denominated bond issued during the period from January 2001 through March 2003.[1] Out of the 33 markets, only 17 had any fixed-rate offerings listed. In addition, only 14 of this subgroup had quotes for the long-dated bond.

---

[1]Table 4.1 was constructed using data from the Bloomberg Professional service. We chose the longest-maturity bond that was issued between January 2001 and March 2003, according to the yield-curve information for each country. The quoted price is the yield quoted on 7 March 2003. If no price is indicated, the country either had no local currency bonds listed on Bloomberg or might have had bonds issued before 2001 for which there was no quoted price. In either of these cases, we assumed that there was no market for fixed-rate instruments in the local currency.

Table 4.1. Terms of Longest-Maturity Fixed-Rate Bonds Issued in Local Currency, 1 January 2001 through 31 March 2003

Country	Term at Issue (years)	Issue Date	Coupon	Rating	Market	Current Yield	Inflation Rate
Argentina	None						36.10%
Bahrain	None						0.40
Brazil	None						15.90
Chile	20	13 Aug 02	6.50%	NR	Domestic	No quote	3.80
China	15	19 Sep 02	2.60	NR	Domestic	No quote	0.20
Colombia	9	28 Jan 02	15.00	NR	Domestic	15.62%	7.20
Czech Republic	10	16 Jan 01	6.95	A1	Domestic	3.88%	−0.40
Egypt	None						3.00
Hungary	15	5 Nov 01	6.75	A1	Domestic	3.88%	4.50
India	30	22 Aug 02	7.95	Ba2	Domestic	6.35%	3.40
Indonesia	8	15 Dec 02	14.50	NR	Domestic	11.85%	7.30
Israel	None						5.10
Jordan	None						0.93
Malaysia	10	20 Sep 01	3.83	A3	Domestic	3.54%	1.60
Mexico	10	3 Nov 03	9.00	NR	Domestic	10.50%	5.50
Morocco	None						2.20
Nigeria	None						13.50
Oman	None						1.00
Pakistan	None						5.00
Peru	None						2.80
Philippines	20	18 Feb 03	13.00	NR	Domestic	13.17%	3.10
Poland	20	13 Apr 02	5.75	A2	Domestic	5.40%	0.50
Russia	None						14.80
Saudi Arabia	None						1.50
Slovakia	10	14 Jan 03	5.00	A3	Domestic	5.03%	6.00
South Africa	7	26 Mar 01	10.00	A2	Domestic	10.35%	12.50
South Korea	10	14 Oct 02	6.14	A3	Domestic	5.14%	3.90
Sri Lanka	15	28 Jan 03	8.50	NR	Domestic	No quote	6.00
Taiwan	30	3 Jul 01	3.63	NR	Domestic	3.41%	−1.50
Thailand	20	28 Mar 01	6.40	Baa1	Domestic	3.95%	1.90
Turkey	None						27.00
Venezuela	None						38.70
Zimbabwe	None						304.50

Note: NR = not rated.
Source: Based on data from Bloomberg.

Note that the absence of a fixed-rate market does not necessarily indicate a high level of risk. A government running a persistent budget surplus may not need to issue public debt, but another government in a high-risk environment could issue debt with a high fixed rate. The total absence of any borrowing at a fixed rate by a government that needs financing indicates a lack of information about the future prospects. For example, the yields on Colombian and Philippine fixed-rate debt are more than 15 percent and 13 percent, respectively, indicating high risk levels. The absence of tradable fixed-rate instruments in countries such as Argentina and Brazil suggests that investors cannot even make a reasonable assessment of the risk.

Finally, in addition to offering a signal about the information available, fixed-rate instruments in any particular market allow investors to estimate the risk-free (default-free) rate of return in the local currency. This risk-free rate can vary greatly—from 3.41 percent in Taiwan (where the inflation rate was –1.5 percent in 2002) to 15.62 percent in Colombia (where the inflation rate was 7.2 percent earlier in the same year). Nevertheless, it can and does serve as a baseline return for the specific market. This market information is fundamental to the valuation process. (This point is discussed further in Chapter 6.)

Company-Specific Information

In addition to determining the amount of general information available in a given market, it is also important to determine the availability and relevance of company-specific information. The common formulations of market efficiency—weak, semi-strong, and strong (each discussed in more detail later in this chapter)—are closely related to company-specific information.

One method that can be used to test the amount of company-specific information available is to divide the return variance of a company's stock price into its company-specific and market components.[2] One would expect markets with a significant amount of company-specific information available to have a substantial amount of the total variance attributable to company-specific factors. In markets without much reliable company-specific information, however, the only reliable information is likely to be for the market as a whole. Thus, in the latter case, the market component of the total risk should be much higher. **Appendix A** shows in more detail how these calculations were performed.

Table 4.2 ranks emerging markets according to the proportion of stock variance attributable to the overall market. Our calculations show that this variance ranges from a low of about 28 percent for South Africa to a high of

---

[2]For a fuller discussion of the relationship between firm-specific information and the firm-specific component of variance in emerging markets, see Morck et al. (2000) and Durnev et al. (2001).

Table 4.2. Proportion of Total Variance Explained by Market Return, 2002

Country	Monthly Standard Deviation of Return	Average Variance Explained by the Market
Egypt	10%	28%
South Africa	7	28
Slovakia	8	30
Mexico	8	31
India	8	33
Brazil	10	35
Peru	6	35
Chile	6	36
Jordan	4	36
Indonesia	13	38
Czech Republic	7	40
Poland	9	41
South Korea	13	41
Argentina	11	43
China	6	43
Thailand	13	43
Colombia	7	45
Philippines	8	45
Israel	7	46
Taiwan	9	47
Zimbabwe	11	47
Hungary	10	50
Turkey	16	50
Venezuela	10	52
Malaysia	10	58
Morocco	04	58
Pakistan	10	60
Russia	17	60
Sri Lanka	8	74
Average	9	44
United States	4	16
Correlation of standard deviation and market portion of total variance		24.88%

Source: Based on data from S&P's Emerging Markets Data Base (EMDB).

74 percent for Sri Lanka, compared with 15 percent for NYSE stocks. The relatively high variance attributable to the overall market suggests that emerging markets have much less relevant company-specific information available than developed markets. The only real surprises in the top half of the table are Egypt and Jordan. These are markets from which a high proportion of company-specific information would not be expected. In the bottom half of markets, the one surprise is Taiwan, which (according to the analysis presented in previous chapters) might be expected to have a substantial amount of company-specific information. The findings in Table 4.2 support our thesis that, in general, less company-specific information is available in emerging markets than in developed ones.

Evaluating Efficiency

The availability of timely and reliable market and company-specific information does not guarantee the efficiency of the market. An additional test of whether or not a market is efficient is an assessment of how market information and company-specific information are used by the market. As noted earlier, most studies of market efficiency in developed markets assume that information is available and the only question is whether and how that information is incorporated into asset prices. The answer to this question defines whether or not a particular market is efficient. Economists describe these relative strengths of market efficiency according to three levels—the weak, semi-strong, and strong forms of market efficiency.

- *Weak-form market efficiency.* In a market exhibiting weak-form market efficiency, asset prices fully reflect past information. Past prices tell investors nothing about future prices. More specifically, weak-form market efficiency rules out trends. Markets in which investors have very short time horizons are the ones most susceptible to violations of weak-form market efficiency.

- *Semi-strong-form market efficiency.* In a market exhibiting semi-strong-form market efficiency, all available public information is fully reflected in current asset prices. This level implies that public information cannot be used to earn excess returns. It also implies that asset prices instantaneously adjust to incorporate new public information. But this form of market efficiency does not rule out the possibility of using private information to earn abnormally high returns.

- *Strong-form market efficiency.* In a market exhibiting strong-form market efficiency, asset prices fully incorporate all available information, both public and private. This level implies that investors cannot earn abnormally high returns, even with inside information.

Empirical studies show that most developed markets, with some variation, exhibit the weak form and semi-strong form of market efficiency. Past prices do not predict future prices, and asset prices adjust quickly to the release of new information (such as earnings announcements and dividend changes). The evidence is much less clear for emerging markets. Given that even developed markets do not exhibit the strong form of market efficiency, it is unlikely to occur in emerging ones. Empirical research has not addressed the semi-strong form of market efficiency for emerging markets. Thus, an exploration of market efficiency in emerging markets today must begin with the weak form of market efficiency.

Evidence supports the existence of weak-form efficiency in several emerging markets. **Exhibit 4.1** summarizes the findings of studies of weak-form efficiency in emerging markets, most of which tested the basic proposition that stock prices follow a random walk. Researchers found weak-form market efficiency in Argentina, Brazil, Chile, China, India, Mexico, South Africa, and Turkey. Other countries have not been studied, or if they have, the evidence suggests that the markets are not efficient.

To apply our own simple test, we used a simple two-period-lagged autoregressive process to evaluate whether past returns predict current returns in emerging markets. The results shown in **Table 4.3** reject the presence of weak-form market efficiency for more than half of the sample. [3]

Information availability affords further perspective on efficiency in emerging markets. In Chapter 2, we identified several countries that equaled or excelled Greece (a market recently reclassified from emerging to developed) in certain attributes, and we found that the difference between this group (called "Group 1") of emerging markets differed from other emerging markets because they had better availability of information. **Table 4.4** combines the grouping information from Chapter 2 with the information and market efficiency issues addressed in this chapter—trading characteristics (Group 1 status in Chapter 2), existence of fixed-rate instruments, relevance of company-specific information in market returns, and research testing the existence of weak-form efficiency. A value of 1 was assigned to each measure that suggested the market would behave efficiently. The markets with the highest scores (i.e., with relatively higher efficiency) are South Korea, South Africa, Mexico, Taiwan, Slovakia, Indonesia, and India. The lowest-scoring markets

---

[3]The analysis used weekly local currency return data from January 1995 through December 2002 for all 31 emerging market countries for which data were available. If the market displayed weak-form efficiency, both coefficients on the one-week-lagged return and the coefficient on the two-week-lagged return should not be significantly different from zero. Note that it is not possible to compare the results reported in Exhibit 4.1 and Table 4.2 because the tests involve different time periods.

Exhibit 4.1. Summary of Studies on Weak-Form Efficiency in Emerging Markets

Country	Article	Weak-Form Efficient
Argentina, Brazil, and Mexico	Ojah et al. (1999)	Yes
	Urrutia (1995)	Yes
Bahrain	None	
Chile	Ojah et al. (1999)	No
	Urrutia (1995)	Yes
China	Laurence et al. (1997)	Yes
	Long et al. (1999)	Yes (A shares)
		No (B shares)
Colombia	None	
Czech Republic	None	
Egypt, Morocco, Nigeria, Zimbabwe	Smith et al. (2002)	No
Hungary	None	
India	Jha (2000)	Yes
Indonesia	None	
Israel	None	
Jordan	None	
Malaysia	Huang (1995)	No
Pakistan	None	
Peru	None	
Philippines	None	
Poland	Gordan et al. (1995)	No
Russia	None	
Saudi Arabia	None	
Slovakia	None	
South Africa	Lamba et al. (2001)	Yes
	Smith et al. (2002)	Yes
South Korea	Huang (1995)	No
	Cheung et al. (1993)	No
	Unro (1997)	No
Sri Lanka	Abeysekera (2001)	No
Taiwan	Cheung et al. (1993)	No
	Unro (1997)	No
Thailand	None	
Turkey	Antoniou et al. (1997)	Yes
	Demirer et al. (2002)	No
Venezuela	None	

Table 4.3. Test of Weak-Form Efficiency in Emerging Markets

Country	One-Week Lag	Two-Week Lag	R^2	Efficiency
Argentina	−0.0036	0.1615***	0.020	N
Bahrain	—	—	—	—
Brazil	−0.0176	0.083	0.001	Y
Chile	0.2412***	−0.0041	0.052	N
China	0.1149**	0.008	0.013	N
Colombia	0.1896***	0.1195**	0.055	N
Czech Republic	0.1237**	0.0603	0.015	N
Egypt	0.0330	−0.013	0.005	Y
Hungary	−0.0616	0.1840***	0.034	N
India	0.0482	−0.0023	0.004	Y
Indonesia	−0.0807	0.0781	0.007	Y
Israel	−0.0246	0.0358	0.005	Y
Jordan	0.0217	0.0166	0.005	Y
Malaysia	0.0264	0.0796	0.001	Y
Mexico	0.0489	−0.0005	0.004	Y
Morocco	0.1420**	0.0234	0.016	N
Nigeria	0.1610***	0.1016*	0.036	N
Pakistan	0.1572***	0.0973*	0.033	N
Peru	0.1155**	0.0126	0.008	N
Philippines	0.0746	0.1760***	0.033	N
Poland	−0.0295	0.1324**	0.017	N
Russia	0.0817	−0.0208	0.001	Y
Slovakia	−0.0629	0.0835	0.005	Y
South Africa	0.0729	0.058	0.003	Y
South Korea	−0.0083	0.0856	0.009	Y
Sri Lanka	0.0911*	0.0492	0.006	N
Taiwan	−0.0216	0.0085	0.006	Y
Thailand	0.0461	0.1724***	0.027	N
Turkey	0.0296	0.1099**	0.007	N
Venezuela	0.0806	0.1319**	0.020	N
Zimbabwe	0.0749	0.0495	0.002	Y
United States	−0.0894	0.0082	0.002	Y

Note: Weekly local currency return data from January 1995 through December 2002.

*Significant at the 10 percent level.
**Significant at the 2 percent level.
***Significant at the 1 percent level.

Source: Based on data from S&P's EMDB.

Table 4.4. Information and Market Efficiency Scores

Country	Trading Characteristics	Fixed Rate	Firm-Specific Information	Weak-Form Efficient	Score
South Korea	1	1	1	1	4
South Africa	1	1	1	1	4
Mexico	1	1	1	1	4
Taiwan	1	1	1	1	4
Slovakia	0	1	1	1	3
Indonesia	0	1	1	1	3
India	0	1	1	1	3
Brazil	1	0	1	1	3
Thailand	0	1	1	0	2
Poland	0	1	1	0	2
Malaysia	0	1	0	1	2
Jordan	0	0	1	1	2
Egypt	0	0	1	1	2
Czech Republic	0	1	1	0	2
China	0	1	1	0	2
Chile	0	1	1	0	2
Zimbabwe	0	0	0	1	1
Venezuela	0	0	0	1	1
Sri Lanka	0	1	0	0	1
Philippines	0	1	0	0	1
Peru	0	0	1	0	1
Israel	0	0	0	1	1
Hungary	0	1	0	0	1
Colombia	0	1	0	0	1
Argentina	0	0	1	0	1
Morocco	0	0	0	0	0
Turkey	0	0	0	0	0
Russia	0	0	0	0	0
Pakistan	0	0	0	0	0

(i.e., comparatively inefficient) are Morocco, Turkey, Russia, and Pakistan. This information is relevant for deciding which type of valuation method is appropriate for valuing investments in a particular market.

Overall, emerging markets do not seem to be efficient. Only about half have a traded long-term fixed-rate instrument in the local currency. All of them have less company-specific information than developed markets. Not surprisingly, only about half of the markets can be considered to exhibit even the weak form of market efficiency. The evidence suggests, however, that these markets vary greatly in efficiency relative to each other.

5. Market Integration and Country versus Sector Factors

Market efficiency, as discussed in the previous chapter, is merely the first major judgment that must be made when analyzing an investment in an emerging market. This chapter focuses on the other major judgments: the level of integration with global markets and the relative importance of country versus industry sector factors in emerging markets. As emerging markets become more integrated with the rest of the world economy, their behavior also should better reflect the behavior of global markets. As discussed in Chapter 3, the speed at which this happens is relevant for the practitioner because the level of integration with world markets determines the appropriate valuation techniques and portfolio decisions. From a valuation standpoint, assumptions about integration are relevant because the risk of the investment—and hence the appropriate cost of capital—changes depending on whether global or local factors are used. From a portfolio-selection standpoint, assumptions about integration determine whether managers should focus on countries, industries, or particular companies.

Although there is evidence of increasing integration between emerging markets and developed markets (e.g., Bekaert, Erb, Harvey, and Viskanta 1997), this chapter shows that emerging markets remain fairly segmented. As a result, the risk of investing in emerging markets likely will depend more on local factors and managers should focus on country factors, rather than global industry factors, in portfolio selection.

Country versus Sector Factors

The relevance of country and sector factors is a critical component in evaluating the performance of individual stocks in emerging markets. Many authors have studied the importance of these factors in developed market economies (for example, Heston and Rouwenhorst 1994, Diermeier and Solnik 2001, and Kritzman and Page 2003, among others). Few have tried to address this question for investable securities in emerging markets as a separate asset class. Given the high growth potential in many emerging economies and the potential for portfolio investments in emerging stock markets, it is time to try to fill the gap in the literature.

In an effort to fill this gap, we used monthly return data from the universe of emerging market stocks (as defined by S&P/IFCI indexes) to evaluate the relative importance of country and industry factors in determining the returns for emerging market securities of 31 emerging market countries between January 1990 and January 2003. The dataset consists of 1,424 companies with a partial or complete return history over the sample period. Using standard industry classification, each company was assigned a one-digit sector code and two-digit industry code. The sample covers nine sectors and 63 two-digit industries.

Table 5.1 and **Table 5.2** show that the distribution of companies is not uniform on either a sector or country basis. Most of the distribution is concentrated in one of three sectors—manufacturing; transportation, communication, and utilities (TCU); and finance. With the exception of manufacturing and finance, not all countries have companies in each of the other sectors. Not surprisingly, given the abundance of labor in many developing countries, the labor-intensive manufacturing sector accounts for nearly half of the companies and more than one-third of the market cap. Companies in the more capital-intensive TCU sector tend to have larger market caps. Although these companies account for less than 10 percent of the sample, they contribute 21 percent of the market cap. Most of these companies were state owned or state controlled in the 1980s, so their significant presence in the S&P/IFCI indexes reveals the significant impact of privatization and liberalization in the 1990s. The number of companies in agriculture, construction, and services is relatively small. Malaysia accounts for most of the companies and most of the market cap in these three sectors because this country has a more even distribution of companies among sectors than most other countries. In Russia, however, the mining sector, which includes oil and gas extraction, accounts for more than 40 percent of the companies and 73 percent of the market cap, whereas Venezuela, which is also rich in oil, has no company investable to foreign investors in this sector. An investment portfolio that tracks the IFCI Russia index is thus largely a bet on the energy sector. In contrast, an investment portfolio that tracks the IFCI India index is mainly a bet on the manufacturing sector.

Substantial differences exist among emerging market countries in both average monthly return and volatility of return, as shown in **Table 5.3**, which summarizes the performance of investable securities in emerging market countries. (All returns are expressed as percent per month and are measured in U.S. dollars.) Russia, Venezuela, Poland, Turkey, and Brazil had the highest returns during the sample period, whereas Egypt, the Czech Republic, and Slovakia performed relatively poorly. Note that value-weighted average returns in emerging markets were substantially lower than equal-weighted

Table 5.1. Industry Composition for Emerging Markets, 1990–2003
(number of sample observations in company months)

Country	AGR	MIN	CON	MFG	TCU	TRA	FIN	SER	OTH	Total
Argentina	63	357	48	1,860	628	13	395	—	201	3,565
Brazil	85	603	—	4,895	2,583	244	720	27	303	9,460
Chile	68	254	—	1,951	1,614	248	665	46	70	4,916
China	46	171	177	2,772	801	58	655	76	196	4,952
Colombia	—	12	—	773	24	106	602	—	—	1,517
Czech Republic	—	24	81	298	269	—	93	—	—	765
Egypt	—	—	93	979	117	—	525	63	—	1,777
Greece	164	85	944	2,833	377	535	1,335	323	—	6,596
Hungary	—	85	—	608	127	49	85	97	144	1,195
India	176	82	—	7,484	637	—	794	620	—	9,793
Indonesia	320	209	—	2,771	283	334	1,122	248	234	5,521
Israel	—	—	106	1,445	76	172	806	27	620	3,252
Jordan	—	37	—	464	—	—	425	22	—	948
Malaysia	1,367	158	1,062	4,073	1,095	457	3,206	776	4,055	16,249
Mexico	—	383	476	3,096	857	1,134	597	299	1,226	8,068
Morocco	—	72	—	213	—	—	423	—	—	708
Pakistan	—	—	—	1,294	463	—	527	—	—	2,284
Peru	24	596	—	686	222	106	347	—	—	1,981
Philippines	—	286	58	744	564	—	1,621	3	533	3,809
Poland	—	63	285	1,442	51	303	715	51	—	2,910
Portugal	12	—	204	764	180	96	885	59	223	2,423
Russia	—	402	—	132	495	12	28	—	—	1,069
Slovakia	—	—	—	171	57	—	57	—	—	285
South Africa	—	1,872	3	1,839	149	904	1,547	267	1,217	7,798
South Korea	—	63	1,253	10,410	1,069	1,214	4,963	465	—	19,437
Sri Lanka	12	—	12	96	—	—	261	25	297	703
Taiwan	145	181	784	8,873	362	256	2,151	236	—	12,988
Thailand	196	403	452	1,923	1,000	450	3,361	219	179	8,183
Turkey	—	—	—	4,206	365	388	1,226	184	329	6,698
Venezuela	—	—	—	831	184	—	252	—	12	1,279
Zimbabwe	36	80	—	42	24	36	272	64	6	560
Emerging markets composite	2,714	6,478	6,038	69,968	14,673	7,115	30,661	4,197	9,845	151,689

Note: AGR = agriculture, forestry, and fishing; MIN = mining; CON = construction; MFG = manufacturing; TCU = transportation, communication, electric, gas, and sanitary services; TRA = wholesale trade and retail trade; FIN = finance, insurance, and real estate; SER = services; OTH = other.

Source: Based on data from S&P's Emerging Markets Data Base (EMDB).

Table 5.2. Average Sector Weights in Value-Weighted Emerging Markets, 1990–2003

Country	AGR	MIN	CON	MFG	TCU	TRA	FIN	SER	OTH	Total
Argentina	0.01%	1.13%	0.00%	0.70%	0.80%	0.01%	0.41%	0.00%	0.05%	3.11
Brazil	0.02	0.89	0.00	3.25	4.43	0.10	1.10	0.01	0.23	10.03
Chile	0.01	0.06	0.00	1.39	1.66	0.25	0.36	0.01	0.04	3.78
China	0.01	0.26	0.03	0.57	1.27	0.00	0.23	0.01	0.03	2.41
Colombia	0.00	0.00	0.00	0.44	0.01	0.02	0.34	0.00	0.00	0.81
Czech Republic	0.00	0.00	0.01	0.06	0.30	0.00	0.04	0.00	0.00	0.41
Egypt	0.00	0.00	0.02	0.17	0.08	0.00	0.13	0.01	0.00	0.41
Greece	0.02	0.03	0.20	1.21	0.54	0.10	1.99	0.08	0.00	4.16
Hungary	0.00	0.13	0.00	0.19	0.32	0.00	0.11	0.02	0.01	0.79
India	0.03	0.00	0.00	1.59	0.17	0.00	0.23	0.29	0.00	2.32
Indonesia	0.03	0.02	0.00	1.15	0.39	0.04	0.19	0.03	0.14	2.00
Israel	0.00	0.00	0.03	0.88	0.10	0.07	0.45	0.01	0.33	1.86
Jordan	0.00	0.00	0.00	0.04	0.00	0.00	0.13	0.00	0.00	0.17
Malaysia	0.84	0.03	0.73	2.19	1.68	0.15	2.28	1.30	2.72	11.93
Mexico	0.00	0.48	0.25	3.55	4.29	1.63	0.84	0.10	1.31	12.46
Morocco	0.00	0.05	0.00	0.06	0.00	0.00	0.38	0.00	0.00	0.49
Pakistan	0.00	0.00	0.00	0.27	0.14	0.00	0.04	0.00	0.00	0.45
Peru	0.00	0.16	0.00	0.17	0.25	0.01	0.18	0.00	0.00	0.77
Philippines	0.00	0.02	0.00	0.38	0.59	0.00	0.66	0.00	0.10	1.76
Poland	0.00	0.03	0.03	0.24	0.12	0.08	0.40	0.01	0.00	0.91
Portugal	0.00	0.00	0.03	0.20	0.28	0.07	0.64	0.01	0.13	1.35
Russia	0.00	1.36	0.00	0.10	0.39	0.00	0.01	0.00	0.00	1.86
Slovakia	0.00	0.00	0.00	0.03	0.00	0.00	0.00	0.00	0.00	0.04
South Africa	0.00	3.46	0.00	2.74	0.50	0.56	3.19	0.14	2.36	12.95
South Korea	0.00	0.00	0.19	4.60	1.50	0.25	1.56	0.09	0.00	8.21
Sri Lanka	0.00	0.00	0.00	0.00	0.00	0.00	0.02	0.00	0.02	0.05
Taiwan	0.00	0.24	0.12	5.49	0.11	0.05	1.96	0.01	0.00	8.01
Thailand	0.00	0.13	0.10	0.42	0.61	0.08	0.91	0.02	0.01	2.32
Turkey	0.00	0.00	0.00	1.19	0.26	0.14	1.59	0.02	0.40	3.59
Venezuela	0.00	0.00	0.00	0.20	0.26	0.00	0.09	0.00	0.00	0.56
Zimbabwe	0.00	0.00	0.00	0.00	0.00	0.00	0.04	0.00	0.00	0.05
Emerging market composite	1.03	8.50	1.74	33.47	21.08	3.62	20.51	2.15	7.90	100.00

Note: AGR = agriculture, forestry, and fishing; MIN = mining; CON = construction; MFG = manufacturing; TCU = transportation, communication, electric, gas, and sanitary services; TRA = wholesale trade and retail trade; FIN = finance, insurance, and real estate; SER = services; OTH = other.

Source: Based on data from S&P's EMDB.

Table 5.3. Equal- and Value-Weighted Performance of Individual Emerging Markets and the IFCI Composite Index, 1990–2003

Country	Equal-Weighted Return		Value-Weighted Return		Currency Return	
	Mean	Standard Deviation	Mean	Standard Deviation	Mean	Standard Deviation
Argentina	1.45%	16.18%	1.41%	15.27%	3.09%	20.48%
Brazil	2.10	17.31	2.12	17.42	9.49	18.24
Chile	1.32	7.73	1.28	7.57	0.61	2.23
Columbia	1.31	11.16	1.29	10.85	1.14	2.27
Mexico	0.90	9.75	1.29	9.86	1.00	4.93
Peru	0.85	9.08	1.05	8.38	0.64	1.46
Venezuela	2.74	17.03	2.78	16.89	2.36	10.10
China	0.45	12.01	−0.32	12.14	0.42	5.26
South Korea	0.65	15.03	0.67	13.67	0.44	5.20
Philippines	0.02	14.50	−0.10	11.02	0.62	3.11
Taiwan	0.49	10.97	0.62	10.77	0.20	1.58
India	0.12	8.84	0.22	8.26	0.44	1.29
Indonesia	0.54	17.97	0.01	14.39	1.52	10.82
Malaysia	0.78	14.48	0.58	10.76	0.25	2.41
Pakistan	0.96	13.14	1.11	12.67	0.82	1.99
Sri Lanka	0.16	11.15	0.21	10.94	0.66	1.38
Thailand	0.38	14.96	0.12	12.55	0.39	3.69
Czech Republic	−0.45	9.11	−0.23	9.06	0.02	3.10
Hungary	1.92	12.91	1.54	11.90	0.85	2.38
Poland	2.46	16.23	2.54	16.26	−0.05	9.52
Russia	3.27	22.87	2.29	20.45	1.41	15.86
Slovakia	−0.44	10.07	−1.29	7.90	0.71	2.51
Portugal	0.86	6.57	1.08	6.81	−0.68	9.99
Greece	1.20	11.53	1.17	11.31	−0.15	8.51
Turkey	2.26	18.82	1.63	18.77	4.44	6.27
Egypt	−1.54	5.88	−1.70	6.94	0.67	2.29
Israel	0.23	8.59	0.42	7.65	0.55	2.32
Jordan	0.88	4.87	0.86	4.31	0.08	0.94
Morocco	0.09	5.28	0.20	4.93	0.10	1.91
South Africa	1.48	9.68	1.08	8.25	0.55	4.05
Zimbabwe	1.68	13.87	2.17	13.23	2.35	6.67
Emerging markets composite	0.98	6.98	0.66	6.61	1.37	2.26

Source: Based on data from S&P's EMDB.

returns, although the equal-weighted returns had greater volatility. These data suggest that, on average, smaller-cap investable stocks in emerging markets had higher returns and higher volatility during the sample period. The average returns in U.S. dollars were positive—even though local currencies depreciated against the U.S. dollar.

The volatility of returns for a sector index is, on average, lower than that for a country index, as shown in **Table 5.4**, which summarizes the performance of nine sectors during the 1990–2003 period. (All returns are expressed as percent per month and are measured in U.S. dollars.) Because the dataset contains more countries than sectors, a plausible explanation is that an average sector portfolio should be more diversified among countries than an average country portfolio is among sectors.

Emerging markets have exhibited low correlations among themselves, as shown in **Table 5.5**. For equal-weighted returns, the average country correlation coefficient is 0.19 during the sample period. For value-weighted returns, the average is 0.21. One possible explanation for the low country correlations might be the difference in industry composition among countries, as shown in Table 5.1 and Table 5.2. Table 5.4, however, shows that this explanation is not supported by the data. The correlations among sectors in emerging markets turn out to be high. The average correlation between equal-weighted sector indexes is 0.83, and the average correlation between value-weighted sector indexes is 0.64.

The data appear to suggest that the returns of an Indian manufacturing company might have little correlation with the returns of a Thai manufacturing company but high correlation with the returns of an Indian bank. The observed high correlations among sectors in emerging markets may simply reflect high intracountry correlations. In other words, they may have a lot to do with high correlations among the returns of companies that belong to different industries but are located in the same country. Thus, low cross-country correlations could be caused by country-specific factors, such as the difference in institutional and legal infrastructures and the difference in macroeconomic policies. If correct, this assumption would imply that stock returns in emerging markets are determined more by country factors than by industry factors. It also would imply that emerging markets as an asset class consist largely of assets located in relatively isolated markets, despite progress toward financial liberalization and integration.

Note, however, that the data suggest some level of regional integration. Although the average cross-country correlation coefficient between equal-weighted returns for all emerging markets is 0.19, the average correlation coefficient for countries in the same region is significantly higher. The

Table 5.4. Equal- and Value-Weighted Sector Performance and Correlations for the IFCI Composite Index, 1990–2003

Sector	Equal-Weighted Return		Value-Weighted Return		Correlation Coefficients (equal weighted below the diagonal, value weighted above)									
	Mean	Std. Dev.	Mean	Std. Dev.	AGR	MIN	CON	MFG	TCU	TRA	FIN	SER	OTH	IND
Agriculture, forestry, and fishing	0.36%	9.16%	0.35%	8.89%		0.43	0.70	0.56	0.46	0.39	0.56	0.69	0.72	0.63
Mining	1.44	7.34	1.54	8.16	0.59		0.45	0.67	0.65	0.50	0.54	0.49	0.65	0.75
Construction	0.85	9.34	0.16	8.99	0.78	0.59		0.72	0.58	0.61	0.60	0.75	0.75	0.74
Manufacturing	0.94	6.64	0.56	6.71	0.69	0.75	0.76		0.78	0.71	0.76	0.69	0.79	0.95
Transportation, communication, electric, gas, and sanitary services	1.85	8.05	1.15	8.43	0.62	0.72	0.63	0.83		0.72	0.60	0.64	0.71	0.87
Wholesale trade and retail trade	1.10	8.21	1.10	7.70	0.60	0.61	0.64	0.73	0.63		0.61	0.55	0.70	0.77
Finance, insurance, and real estate	0.98	8.37	0.55	7.29	0.76	0.70	0.77	0.87	0.76	0.79		0.65	0.76	0.85
Services	0.83	9.08	0.64	8.73	0.71	0.63	0.72	0.76	0.71	0.68	0.82		0.81	0.77
Other	0.85	9.38	0.37	7.84	0.87	0.68	0.78	0.75	0.71	0.68	0.80	0.80		0.89
Emerging markets composite	0.98	6.98	0.66	6.61	0.79	0.79	0.82	0.97	0.86	0.80	0.95	0.85	0.86	

Note: AGR = agriculture, forestry, and fishing; MIN = mining; CON = construction; MFG = manufacturing; TCU = transportation, communication, electric, gas, and sanitary services; TRA = wholesale trade and retail trade; FIN = finance, insurance, and real estate; SER = services; OTH = other; IND = S&P/IFCI Emerging Markets Composite Index.

Source: Based on data from S&P's EMDB.

Table 5.5. Correlations among Emerging Market Countries, 1990–2003
(equal-weighted below the diagonal, value-weighted above)

	ARG	BRZ	CHL	COL	MEX	PER	VEN	CHN	KOR	PHL	TAI	IND	INS	MAL	PAK	SLK	THA
ARG		0.26	0.35	0.17	0.43	0.43	0.19	0.34	0.17	0.28	0.26	0.17	0.11	0.16	0.17	0.21	0.22
BRZ	0.18		0.38	0.32	0.40	0.46	0.08	0.32	0.22	0.24	0.31	0.34	0.26	0.15	0.25	0.35	0.20
CHL	0.36	0.37		0.23	0.42	0.54	0.06	0.34	0.31	0.41	0.40	0.47	0.36	0.36	0.27	0.30	0.38
COL	0.16	0.32	0.23		0.13	0.35	0.33	0.10	0.17	0.25	0.16	0.19	0.25	0.15	0.35	0.27	0.13
MEX	0.34	0.40	0.43	0.13		0.49	0.12	0.42	0.26	0.36	0.32	0.30	0.28	0.33	0.24	0.30	0.36
PER	0.48	0.46	0.54	0.35	0.49		0.19	0.18	0.15	0.34	0.27	0.15	0.30	0.19	0.20	0.25	0.23
VEN	0.14	0.08	0.05	0.33	0.10	0.19		0.30	0.13	0.09	0.12	0.21	0.10	0.14	0.09	0.25	0.04
CHN	0.19	0.25	0.22	0.00	0.26	0.13	0.28		0.15	0.38	0.46	0.29	0.30	0.55	0.20	0.18	0.35
KOR	0.17	0.22	0.30	0.28	0.21	0.15	0.13	0.04		0.31	0.34	0.23	0.34	0.27	0.11	0.25	0.57
PHL	0.23	0.24	0.37	0.21	0.28	0.27	0.04	0.29	0.33		0.47	0.17	0.60	0.57	0.15	0.09	0.66
TAI	0.24	0.31	0.35	0.20	0.28	0.23	0.14	0.29	0.21	0.41		0.16	0.30	0.47	0.18	0.11	0.46
IND	0.04	0.34	0.39	0.15	0.24	0.09	0.18	0.24	0.18	0.18	0.16		0.23	0.26	0.39	0.36	0.19
INS	0.13	0.26	0.36	0.25	0.26	0.30	0.13	0.30	0.32	0.59	0.21	0.27		0.51	0.18	0.28	0.51
MAL	0.09	0.15	0.30	0.12	0.23	0.19	0.14	0.43	0.29	0.53	0.39	0.22	0.60		0.27	0.19	0.64
PAK	0.18	0.25	0.28	0.36	0.26	0.22	0.06	0.15	0.12	0.08	0.15	0.36	0.18	0.27		0.51	0.24
SLK	0.24	0.35	0.35	0.28	0.30	0.28	0.22	0.12	0.25	0.07	0.01	0.39	0.28	0.18	0.55		0.15
THA	0.17	0.20	0.27	0.13	0.27	0.23	0.01	0.26	0.56	0.67	0.38	0.18	0.52	0.59	0.21	0.15	
CZR	0.20	0.41	0.27	0.22	0.24	0.20	0.29	0.23	0.20	0.21	0.24	0.38	0.26	0.19	0.32	0.35	0.18
HUN	0.36	0.41	0.39	0.29	0.50	0.33	0.06	0.10	0.15	0.24	0.16	0.29	0.26	0.15	0.24	0.39	0.22
POL	0.23	0.36	0.25	0.21	0.41	0.20	0.18	0.25	0.13	0.18	0.15	0.29	0.24	0.31	0.19	0.31	0.21
RUS	0.32	0.55	0.67	0.52	0.51	0.51	0.01	0.30	0.34	0.36	0.33	0.21	0.56	0.35	0.47	0.37	0.37
SLO	-0.18	-0.04	-0.12	-0.17	0.01	-0.14	-0.02	0.08	-0.06	-0.19	-0.23	0.10	-0.06	-0.08	-0.06	-0.03	-0.12
POR	0.09	0.27	0.20	0.12	0.14	0.18	-0.09	0.05	0.14	0.34	0.16	0.21	0.31	0.16	-0.03	0.31	0.30
GRE	-0.03	0.26	0.21	0.06	0.11	0.22	0.02	0.04	0.11	0.15	0.15	0.35	0.20	0.11	0.05	0.28	0.12
TUR	-0.01	0.25	0.21	0.17	0.20	0.16	0.02	0.05	0.12	0.04	0.18	0.16	0.08	0.08	0.32	0.24	0.12
EGP	0.06	0.01	0.24	0.11	0.03	0.10	0.08	0.01	0.10	0.05	0.20	0.31	0.08	0.18	0.23	0.02	0.17
ISR	0.19	0.46	0.48	0.15	0.43	0.28	0.13	0.16	0.13	0.10	0.09	0.37	0.24	0.19	0.35	0.24	0.04
JOR	0.02	0.07	0.15	0.16	0.15	0.19	-0.03	-0.18	0.10	0.03	-0.06	0.14	0.09	0.04	0.21	0.23	0.11
MOR	-0.17	-0.18	-0.17	-0.26	-0.29	-0.03	-0.25	-0.01	-0.10	-0.03	0.08	0.13	-0.07	-0.09	-0.23	-0.01	-0.03
SAF	0.26	0.29	0.32	0.08	0.34	0.24	0.14	0.21	0.23	0.41	0.29	0.17	0.33	0.33	0.25	0.22	0.44
ZIM	0.33	0.27	0.34	0.28	0.26	0.26	0.15	0.20	0.37	0.22	0.22	0.26	0.17	0.15	0.14	0.12	0.24
IND	0.32	0.53	0.60	0.35	0.55	0.42	0.16	0.42	0.63	0.64	0.58	0.45	0.64	0.69	0.41	0.42	0.73

Table 5.5. Correlations among Emerging Market Countries, 1990–2003 (continued)

(equal-weighted below the diagonal, value-weighted above)

	CZR	HUN	POL	RUS	SLO	POR	GRE	TUR	EGP	ISR	JOR	MOR	SAF	ZIM	IND
ARG	0.28	0.35	0.27	0.32	−0.22	0.15	0.06	0.05	0.16	0.21	−0.08	−0.09	0.32	0.34	0.43
BRZ	0.33	0.49	0.38	0.59	−0.16	0.29	0.32	0.27	0.09	0.43	0.07	−0.18	0.36	0.30	0.58
CHL	0.29	0.43	0.28	0.67	−0.10	0.19	0.25	0.19	0.34	0.43	0.16	−0.15	0.45	0.34	0.60
COL	0.10	0.24	0.19	0.43	−0.07	0.08	0.14	0.18	0.20	0.11	0.11	−0.30	0.08	0.31	0.29
MEX	0.34	0.51	0.40	0.60	−0.02	0.12	0.08	0.19	0.19	0.41	0.05	−0.26	0.46	0.28	0.73
PER	0.24	0.39	0.23	0.44	−0.09	0.18	0.18	0.14	0.11	0.30	0.11	−0.10	0.30	0.32	0.49
VEN	0.33	0.11	0.21	0.15	−0.10	−0.03	0.10	0.04	0.18	0.27	0.02	−0.27	0.19	0.24	0.17
CHN	0.38	0.23	0.28	0.33	0.02	0.04	0.05	0.18	0.13	0.29	−0.11	−0.05	0.41	0.24	0.56
KOR	0.22	0.19	0.21	0.28	0.00	0.22	0.19	0.18	0.12	0.07	0.08	−0.09	0.38	0.32	0.50
PHL	0.22	0.26	0.27	0.47	−0.25	0.31	0.15	0.12	0.15	0.16	0.00	−0.15	0.58	0.26	0.61
TAI	0.31	0.21	0.20	0.49	−0.18	0.19	0.17	0.23	0.22	0.18	0.03	−0.03	0.39	0.24	0.61
IND	0.35	0.38	0.28	0.22	0.03	0.20	0.28	0.16	0.37	0.38	0.11	0.10	0.18	0.31	0.43
INS	0.23	0.30	0.22	0.58	0.01	0.35	0.20	0.13	0.09	0.15	0.07	−0.10	0.36	0.25	0.54
MAL	0.32	0.23	0.31	0.31	−0.01	0.17	0.10	0.11	0.21	0.14	0.05	−0.12	0.42	0.20	0.63
PAK	0.31	0.23	0.16	0.35	0.05	−0.05	0.12	0.28	0.17	0.30	0.20	−0.19	0.21	0.18	0.37
SLK	0.31	0.38	0.27	0.37	0.03	0.30	0.37	0.24	−0.02	0.26	0.27	−0.04	0.24	0.16	0.41
THA	0.22	0.18	0.26	0.38	−0.06	0.26	0.10	0.16	0.26	0.02	0.09	−0.06	0.60	0.23	0.64
CZR		0.61	0.54	0.37	0.08	0.39	0.31	0.29	0.20	0.16	−0.01	−0.15	0.31	0.17	0.50
HUN	0.47		0.50	0.52	0.08	0.57	0.19	0.29	0.26	0.20	0.09	−0.10	0.28	0.18	0.53
POL	0.45	0.48		0.36	0.12	0.43	0.15	0.19	0.34	0.28	0.27	−0.10	0.32	0.27	0.48
RUS	0.32	0.54	0.36		0.01	0.46	0.08	0.54	0.21	0.26	0.16	−0.25	0.50	0.25	0.71
SLO	0.18	0.09	0.11	0.03		0.03	−0.06	0.06	0.03	−0.01	0.12	0.10	0.02	−0.08	−0.01
POR	0.35	0.48	0.44	0.29	−0.03		0.42	0.18	−0.08	0.11	0.11	−0.03	0.33	0.13	0.40
GRE	0.18	0.41	0.22	0.13	0.01	0.44		0.28	0.18	0.33	0.24	0.21	0.28	0.10	0.35
TUR	0.18	0.27	0.21	0.40	0.06	0.17	0.23		0.08	0.40	0.08	−0.23	0.20	0.09	0.42
EGP	0.11	0.11	0.33	0.11	0.07	0.04	−0.06	0.23		0.12	0.16	0.09	0.33	0.20	0.29
ISR	0.25	0.17	0.32	0.33	0.17	0.06	0.31	0.34	0.05		0.19	−0.07	0.21	0.14	0.42
JOR	−0.01	0.14	0.34	0.17	0.00	0.07	0.15	0.16	0.14	0.18		−0.07	0.00	0.05	0.15
MOR	−0.20	−0.12	−0.11	−0.22	0.03	−0.05	0.29	−0.24	0.09	−0.06	0.03		0.03	−0.24	−0.15
SAF	0.22	0.25	0.25	0.28	−0.02	0.27	0.22	0.24	0.13	0.06	0.04	0.04		0.18	0.70
ZIM	0.35	0.21	0.28	0.23	−0.12	0.22	0.07	0.12	0.20	0.09	0.09	−0.26	0.18		0.37
IND	0.43	0.44	0.44	0.63	−0.07	0.40	0.37	0.37	0.20	0.40	0.16	−0.11	0.54	0.40	

Notes: Shaded cells group countries by regions. See Table 5.3 for full country names. IND = S&P/IFCI Emerging Markets.

Source: Based on data from S&P's EMDB.

coefficient for Latin America is 0.29; for Asia, 0.29; and for Europe, 0.28. These data do not contradict the hypothesis of isolated markets because country-specific factors can be expected to be similar among neighbors. Rather, the implication is that as long as emerging markets generally consist of assets located in relatively isolated markets, the region in which the country is located will have an effect on its performance.

Estimating Country and Industry Effects

To formally assess the relative importance of country and industry factors in determining the returns of emerging market securities, we used the Heston and Rouwenhorst (1994) method to decompose the return on a security into country and industry components through a dummy variable regression specification. A detailed description of the date and the empirical model used can be found in **Appendix B**.

The regression analysis included 31 country effects and 9 industry effects, from which we estimated equal- and value-weighted pure country returns and pure industry returns. The 36-month moving averages of the equal-weighted and value-weighted returns on pure country portfolios for a small group of countries are shown in Panel A and Panel B of **Figure 5.1**. (A pure country portfolio is a country portfolio that is rebalanced to be fully diversified among industries in the IFCI emerging markets; see Appendix B for more discussion on how we constructed these portfolios.)

One prominent feature of Figure 5.1 is the large cross-country variation in pure country returns around S&P/IFCI benchmark returns, as computed using all available S&P/IFCI return data. The monthly pure country returns in Argentina were much higher than the emerging market benchmark returns in the early 1990s because Argentina had recovered from a deep economic crisis in the late 1980s. In 2002, however, Argentine returns fell sharply below the benchmark returns after the devaluation of the Argentine peso. The Asian financial crisis that started in the fall of 1997 inflicted sharp losses on South Korean stocks, but Argentina, South Africa, and Turkey were largely unscathed. Russia, with a relatively young stock market concentrated in oil and energy stocks, gained in the early 2000s as the average world oil price rose sharply from a low of less than $10 a barrel in January 1999.

Consider the 36-month equal- and value-weighted moving-average returns for pure sector portfolios shown in Panel A and Panel B of **Figure 5.2**. A pure industry portfolio is an industry portfolio that is rebalanced to be fully diversified among countries in the IFCI emerging markets (see Appendix B for more discussion). For comparison, each figure also shows the returns for the IFCI composite index. The transportation, telecommunications, and utilities stocks, which make up one sector, outperformed all other sectors in the early

Figure 5.1.   Selected Equal- and Value-Weighted Pure Country Returns, January 1993–January 2003
(36-month moving average)

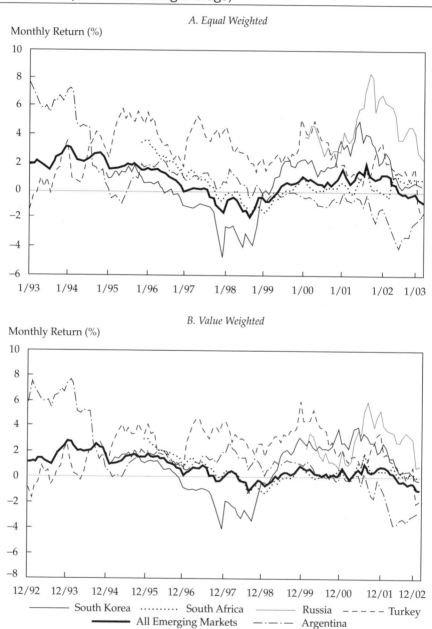

Source: Based on data from S&P's EMDB.

Figure 5.2. Equal- and Value-Weighted Pure Sector Returns, December 1992–December 2002
(36-month moving average)

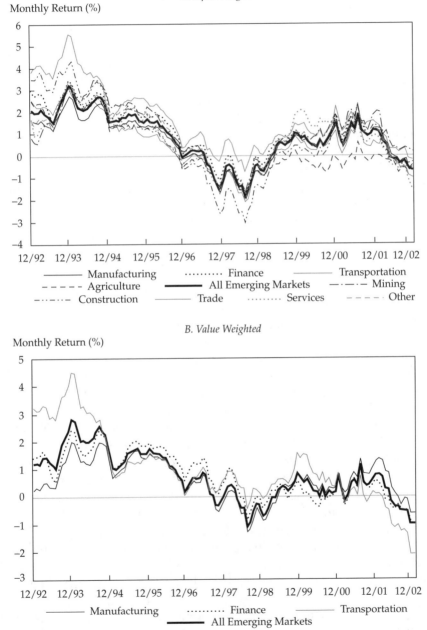

A. Equal Weighted

Monthly Return (%)

——— Manufacturing	·········· Finance	——— Transportation
– – – – – Agriculture	—— All Emerging Markets	—·—·— Mining
—·——·—· Construction	——— Trade	·········· Services	– – – – Other

B. Value Weighted

Monthly Return (%)

——— Manufacturing	·········· Finance	——— Transportation
	—— All Emerging Markets	

Source: Based on data from S&P's EMDB.

and mid-1990s but became the second worst performer by January 2003, the last month in our sample. In contrast, the mining sector, which included many oil and natural gas stocks, became the best-performing sector, as oil prices rose sharply in the last few years in our sample.

The observed intercountry and interindustry variance in the estimated returns for pure country and industry portfolios clearly indicates that country and industry factors are important sources of variance of company returns. But visible differences also appear in the size of estimated country and industry effects. A comparison of the information shown in Figure 5.1 through Figure 5.2 clearly highlights the fact that intercountry variance in the estimated pure country returns is greater than interindustry variance in the estimated pure industry returns.

Relative Importance

Consider the summary statistics for the estimated pure country industry returns, as shown in **Table 5.6, Table 5.7** and **Table 5.8**. Consistent with the findings in Figure 5.1 and Figure 5.2, Table 5.6 shows that cross-sectional variance is greater for the average pure country returns than for the average pure industry returns. Table 5.6 shows that the equal-weighted average monthly return on a pure country portfolio ranges from –0.68 percent for Egypt to 2.47 percent for Venezuela, whereas Table 5.8 shows that the equal-weighted average monthly return on a pure industry portfolio ranges from 0.76 percent for agriculture, forestry, and fishing to 1.69 percent for transportation, telecommunications, and utilities. A comparison of value-weighted average pure country and industry returns yields similar results.

Comparing the entries in Table 5.6 and Table 5.7 with those in Tables 5.3 and 5.5 shows that industry effects also have little impact on average country return/volatility and intercountry correlations. The country performance and return characteristics in Tables 5.3 and 5.5 appear to be explained largely by the country-specific effects in Table 5.6. The effects of industry specialization are small for most countries but appear to be more important for those countries where listed stocks are highly concentrated in specific industries. A good example is Russia, a country where most investable market cap is concentrated in the mining sector. Although Russia recorded a value-weighted monthly excess return of 1.63 percent (the Russian return of 2.29 percent in Table 5.3 minus the 0.66 percent S&P/IFCI emerging markets benchmark return), the contribution made by the country effect is only 0.06 percent (0.72 percent in Table 5.6 minus the 0.66 percent S&P/IFCI emerging markets benchmark return). Part of Russia's positive excess return can be explained by its specialization in oil and gas stocks, which performed well in the late 1990s and the early 2000s.

Table 5.6. Estimated Pure Country Returns after Taking into Account Eight Sector Effects, 1990–2003

Country	Equal-Weighted Return		Value-Weighted Return	
	Mean	Std. Dev.	Mean	Std. Dev.
Argentina	1.52	16.19	1.55	15.84
Brazil	2.15	17.32	2.22	17.52
Chile	1.06	7.80	1.23	7.65
Colombia	1.11	10.07	1.12	10.01
Mexico	1.00	9.84	1.40	9.83
Peru	0.58	8.04	0.64	7.49
Venezuela	2.47	16.15	2.44	16.11
China	0.39	10.56	−0.14	10.56
South Korea	0.56	13.76	0.58	12.51
Philippines	−0.11	14.27	−0.18	10.89
Taiwan	0.49	10.58	0.57	10.18
India	0.14	7.83	0.18	7.05
Indonesia	0.55	17.52	0.11	14.07
Malaysia	0.79	14.38	0.67	10.91
Pakistan	0.72	11.81	0.89	11.57
Sri Lanka	0.04	9.05	0.22	8.73
Thailand	0.29	14.90	0.16	12.56
Czech Republic	−0.28	7.62	−0.10	7.52
Hungary	1.48	11.48	1.17	10.47
Poland	1.96	14.29	2.00	14.41
Russia	1.43	15.78	0.72	14.70
Slovakia	−0.18	5.99	−0.51	4.71
Portugal	0.56	5.48	0.72	5.70
Greece	1.22	11.43	1.24	11.04
Turkey	2.36	18.91	1.86	18.79
Egypt	−0.68	4.00	−0.71	4.79
Israel	0.11	5.78	0.23	5.21
Jordan	0.85	4.73	0.75	4.32
Morocco	0.01	3.80	0.09	3.60
South Africa	1.06	8.33	0.74	7.20
Zimbabwe	0.99	11.14	1.36	10.53
Emerging Markets Composite	0.97	6.94	0.66	6.61

Table 5.7. Correlations among Emerging Market Countries Taking into Account Eight Sector Effects, 1990–2003

Country	ARG	BRZ	CHL	COL	MEX	PER	VEN	CHN	KOR	PHL	TAI	IND	INS	MAL	PAK	SLK	THA
ARG		0.28	0.29	0.17	0.42	0.28	0.15	0.24	0.12	0.26	0.28	0.12	0.13	0.15	0.15	0.09	0.24
BRZ	0.19		0.38	0.24	0.40	0.31	0.07	0.20	0.15	0.23	0.26	0.22	0.23	0.15	0.19	0.19	0.22
CHL	0.30	0.36		0.18	0.40	0.46	0.07	0.28	0.28	0.42	0.38	0.38	0.37	0.36	0.23	0.20	0.39
COL	0.15	0.24	0.19		0.13	0.27	0.28	0.08	0.13	0.21	0.16	0.15	0.23	0.10	0.38	0.16	0.13
MEX	0.34	0.38	0.42	0.16		0.44	0.11	0.37	0.24	0.36	0.34	0.26	0.29	0.32	0.21	0.23	0.36
PER	0.29	0.27	0.45	0.27	0.46		0.13	0.20	0.17	0.30	0.28	0.15	0.30	0.21	0.19	0.23	0.23
VEN	0.12	0.10	0.05	0.20	0.10	0.16		0.22	0.11	0.08	0.10	0.15	0.09	0.15	0.09	0.17	0.04
CHN	0.12	0.16	0.20	0.00	0.24	0.16	0.22		0.15	0.34	0.46	0.27	0.23	0.54	0.18	0.13	0.34
KOR	0.11	0.17	0.28	0.21	0.19	0.14	0.10	0.04		0.29	0.31	0.20	0.33	0.25	0.10	0.20	0.56
PHL	0.24	0.19	0.37	0.17	0.27	0.28	0.04	0.29	0.31		0.45	0.16	0.58	0.55	0.15	0.03	0.65
TAI	0.24	0.22	0.33	0.18	0.28	0.24	0.12	0.28	0.21	0.40		0.25	0.29	0.45	0.18	0.06	0.45
IND	0.03	0.21	0.33	0.12	0.22	0.12	0.14	0.24	0.17	0.17	0.16		0.23	0.25	0.32	0.36	0.18
INS	0.13	0.23	0.39	0.24	0.25	0.36	0.11	0.31	0.31	0.58	0.22	0.28		0.50	0.15	0.15	0.51
MAL	0.10	0.13	0.35	0.11	0.21	0.20	0.14	0.43	0.27	0.52	0.38	0.22	0.59		0.25	0.13	0.62
PAK	0.15	0.20	0.25	0.37	0.25	0.19	0.06	0.14	0.11	0.07	0.14	0.32	0.19	0.27		0.45	0.24
SLK	0.10	0.21	0.19	0.18	0.24	0.26	0.15	0.11	0.20	0.01	-0.03	0.36	0.22	0.12	0.44		0.08
THA	0.19	0.17	0.35	0.11	0.27	0.18	0.01	0.25	0.53	0.67	0.36	0.17	0.51	0.59	0.20	0.09	
CZR	0.12	0.25	0.22	0.17	0.21	0.20	0.20	0.22	0.22	0.20	0.20	0.35	0.27	0.18	0.27	0.32	0.17
HUN	0.21	0.25	0.30	0.22	0.45	0.35	0.03	0.10	0.15	0.22	0.16	0.29	0.27	0.14	0.21	0.36	0.21
POL	0.12	0.22	0.18	0.16	0.36	0.20	0.13	0.25	0.13	0.15	0.15	0.29	0.23	0.29	0.17	0.28	0.19
RUS	0.15	0.30	0.42	0.31	0.31	0.35	-0.01	0.28	0.33	0.31	0.25	0.17	0.54	0.31	0.32	0.28	0.33
SLO	-0.06	-0.02	-0.06	-0.09	0.01	-0.09	0.00	0.06	-0.04	-0.14	-0.14	0.08	-0.04	-0.05	-0.04	-0.02	-0.09
POR	0.10	0.23	0.14	0.10	0.11	0.15	-0.09	-0.01	0.09	0.28	0.09	0.10	0.20	0.11	-0.04	0.17	0.23
GRE	-0.01	0.27	0.20	0.05	0.12	0.18	0.02	0.03	0.09	0.14	0.13	0.28	0.17	0.10	0.05	0.20	0.11
TUR	-0.01	0.25	0.20	0.15	0.20	0.16	0.02	0.05	0.11	0.03	0.18	0.14	0.08	0.08	0.29	0.18	0.12
EGP	0.04	0.01	0.17	0.10	0.03	0.06	0.07	-0.01	0.06	0.04	0.16	0.23	0.07	0.17	0.16	-0.02	0.12
ISR	0.08	0.25	0.29	0.06	0.28	0.20	0.05	0.12	0.10	0.04	0.06	0.27	0.19	0.14	0.21	0.16	0.01
JOR	0.03	0.08	0.11	0.14	0.15	0.10	-0.02	-0.16	0.06	0.04	-0.05	0.11	0.04	0.02	0.20	0.16	0.08
MOR	-0.10	-0.12	-0.15	-0.22	-0.19	-0.05	-0.13	0.01	-0.15	-0.05	-0.05	0.12	-0.12	-0.10	-0.18	-0.01	-0.05
SAF	0.15	0.18	0.24	0.01	0.29	0.27	0.07	0.24	0.21	0.39	0.28	0.20	0.32	0.31	0.17	0.15	0.42
ZIM	0.15	0.14	0.26	0.16	0.21	0.24	0.10	0.22	0.31	0.19	0.18	0.25	0.14	0.14	0.11	0.09	0.21
IND	0.33	0.53	0.60	0.30	0.54	0.40	0.16	0.39	0.58	0.63	0.55	0.42	0.62	0.68	0.37	0.31	0.72

Notes: Shaded cells group countries by regions. See Table 5.6 for full country names. IND = S&P/IFCI Emerging Markets Composite Index.

Source: Based on data from S&P's EMDB.

Table 5.7. Correlations among Emerging Market Countries Taking into Account Eight Sector Effects, 1990–2003 (continued)

Country	CZR	HUN	POL	RUS	SLO	POR	GRE	TUR	EGP	ISR	JOR	MOR	SAF	ZIM	IND
ARG	0.16	0.24	0.16	0.21	-0.06	0.17	0.10	0.06	0.08	0.10	0.00	-0.06	0.23	0.16	0.53
BRZ	0.19	0.31	0.23	0.33	-0.05	0.27	0.32	0.27	0.04	0.21	0.05	-0.09	0.25	0.15	0.57
CHL	0.26	0.35	0.21	0.42	-0.03	0.16	0.26	0.19	0.21	0.22	0.09	-0.13	0.37	0.24	0.57
COL	0.10	0.18	0.14	0.24	0.02	0.12	0.12	0.16	0.16	0.03	0.11	-0.21	0.03	0.18	0.27
MEX	0.28	0.44	0.34	0.40	0.01	0.10	0.10	0.19	0.12	0.24	0.07	-0.16	0.42	0.22	0.75
PER	0.24	0.42	0.24	0.31	-0.03	0.17	0.13	0.16	0.05	0.19	0.06	-0.07	0.31	0.29	0.44
VEN	0.23	0.05	0.13	0.05	-0.01	-0.03	0.11	0.04	0.09	0.09	-0.01	-0.14	0.10	0.15	0.17
CHN	0.35	0.21	0.29	0.29	0.02	-0.02	0.03	0.15	0.05	0.19	-0.11	-0.04	0.42	0.23	0.51
KOR	0.24	0.19	0.22	0.27	-0.02	0.16	0.14	0.16	0.09	0.03	0.05	-0.06	0.38	0.29	0.47
PHL	0.19	0.22	0.22	0.31	-0.12	0.25	0.11	0.11	0.09	0.07	-0.07	-0.16	0.48	0.18	0.59
TAI	0.26	0.22	0.21	0.36	-0.10	0.13	0.13	0.21	0.11	0.11	-0.01	-0.02	0.41	0.18	0.56
IND	0.31	0.37	0.30	0.16	0.03	0.13	0.21	0.14	0.15	0.27	0.10	0.10	0.22	0.28	0.39
INS	0.27	0.32	0.21	0.51	0.03	0.25	0.15	0.11	0.27	0.10	-0.04	-0.16	0.34	0.18	0.51
MAL	0.30	0.20	0.28	0.25	0.02	0.12	0.08	0.09	0.08	0.08	0.00	-0.15	0.37	0.15	0.60
PAK	0.29	0.20	0.15	0.25	0.05	-0.01	0.10	0.25	0.16	0.16	0.21	-0.14	0.17	0.15	0.34
SLK	0.27	0.37	0.25	0.27	0.00	0.19	0.25	0.18	0.11	0.19	0.21	0.00	0.18	0.13	0.35
THA	0.21	0.16	0.23	0.32	-0.02	0.20	0.10	0.16	-0.03	-0.02	0.04	-0.08	0.55	0.19	0.64
CZR		0.48	0.36	0.33	0.09	0.18	0.20	0.21	0.08	0.08	-0.02	-0.14	0.26	0.15	0.46
HUN	0.48		0.49	0.36	0.05	0.42	0.15	0.26	0.11	0.12	0.03	-0.09	0.29	0.16	0.50
POL	0.36	0.49		0.16	0.05	0.36	0.12	0.18	0.17	0.13	0.22	-0.04	0.32	0.20	0.48
RUS	0.33	0.36	0.16		0.02	0.20	0.06	0.38	0.12	0.24	0.01	-0.28	0.42	0.19	0.64
SLO	0.09	0.05	0.05	0.02		-0.03	-0.04	0.06	0.08	-0.01	0.07	0.06	0.04	-0.09	0.31
POR	0.18	0.42	0.36	0.20	-0.03		0.39	0.12	-0.01	0.03	0.08	0.01	0.16	0.10	0.38
GRE	0.20	0.15	0.12	0.06	-0.04	0.39		0.24	-0.05	0.23	0.22	0.17	0.17	0.05	0.37
TUR	0.21	0.26	0.18	0.38	0.06	0.12	0.24		0.15	0.28	0.08	-0.11	0.24	0.08	0.39
EGP	0.08	0.11	0.17	0.12	0.08	-0.01	-0.05	0.15		0.06	0.02	0.09	0.13	0.17	0.38
ISR	0.08	0.12	0.13	0.24	-0.01	0.03	0.23	0.28	0.06		0.11	-0.06	0.06	0.05	0.41
JOR	-0.02	0.03	0.22	0.01	0.07	0.08	0.22	0.08	0.02	0.11		0.07	0.00	0.03	0.10
MOR	-0.14	-0.09	-0.04	-0.28	0.06	0.01	0.17	-0.11	0.09	-0.06	0.07		0.07	-0.17	0.28
SAF	0.26	0.29	0.32	0.42	0.04	0.16	0.17	0.24	0.13	0.06	0.00	0.07		0.15	0.52
ZIM	0.15	0.16	0.20	0.19	-0.09	0.10	0.05	0.08	0.17	0.05	0.03	-0.17	0.15		0.36
IND	0.46	0.50	0.48	0.64	0.31	0.38	0.37	0.39	0.38	0.41	0.10	0.28	0.52	0.36	

Notes: Shaded cells group countries by regions. See Table 5.6 for full country names. IND = S&P/IFCI Emerging Markets Composite Index.

Source: Based on data from S&P's EMDB.

Table 5.8. Estimated Sector Returns after Considering Effects from 31 Emerging Market Countries, 1990–2003

| Sector | Equal-Weighted Return | | Value-Weighted Return | | Correlation Coefficients (equal weighted below the diagonal, value weighted above) | | | | | | | | | |
	Mean	Std. Dev.	Mean	Std. Dev.	AGR	MIN	CON	MFG	TCU	TRA	FIN	SER	OTH	EM
Agriculture, forestry, and fishing	0.76	6.69	0.57	7.90		0.53	0.63	0.70	0.65	0.55	0.67	0.66	0.72	0.85
Mining	1.01	7.40	0.78	6.89	0.68		0.66	0.70	0.56	0.60	0.69	0.56	0.74	0.84
Construction	1.08	8.43	0.55	8.06	0.76	0.72		0.86	0.73	0.73	0.84	0.74	0.86	0.90
Manufacturing	0.79	6.67	0.48	6.50	0.82	0.81	0.88		0.81	0.79	0.89	0.79	0.92	0.99
Transportation, communication, and utilities	1.69	7.75	1.00	7.77	0.79	0.72	0.80	0.88		0.70	0.81	0.80	0.81	0.92
Wholesale trade and retail trade	0.95	7.64	0.59	7.06	0.70	0.64	0.75	0.82	0.73		0.80	0.68	0.82	0.85
Finance, insurance, and real estate	1.27	7.96	0.78	7.33	0.81	0.79	0.85	0.93	0.87	0.80		0.83	0.94	0.97
Services	0.87	8.27	0.82	8.22	0.69	0.74	0.73	0.83	0.79	0.74	0.83		0.85	0.86
Other	0.88	7.79	0.46	7.85	0.81	0.80	0.87	0.95	0.87	0.81	0.94	0.85		0.97
Emerging markets composite	0.97	6.94	0.66	6.61	0.85	0.84	0.90	0.99	0.92	0.85	0.97	0.86	0.97	

Note: AGR = agriculture, forestry, and fishing; MIN = mining; CON = construction; MFG = manufacturing; TCU = transportation, communication, electric, gas, and sanitary services; TRA = wholesale trade and retail trade; FIN = finance, insurance, and real estate; SER = services; OTH = other.

Source: Based on data from S&P's EMDB.

By controlling for country effects, one can construct pure industry portfolios that are fully diversified on a country basis. A comparison of the statistics of the pure industry returns in Table 5.6 with statistics of the raw industry returns in Table 5.4 shows that an increase in country diversification would have reduced the volatility of value-weighted industry portfolios and increased the average correlation between industry portfolios.

To ascertain the statistical significance of country and industry factors in explaining cross-sectional differences in volatility, we conducted F-tests in the ordinary least squares (OLS) regression outlined in Appendix B. The results are presented in **Table 5.9**. The tests clearly show that country effects are statistically significant at both the 5 percent and 1 percent level in explaining monthly cross-sectional variance in stock returns. But for more than half of the tests done with nine one-digit industry effects, the data fail to reject the null hypothesis that industry effects are jointly statistically insignificant. The same is true in about one-quarter of the tests done with 63 one-digit industry effects. These test results clearly suggest that country factors are statistically more significant than industry factors in explaining cross-sectional variance in emerging market stock returns.

Clearly, country factors should have more explanatory power than industry factors in the OLS regression outlined in Appendix B. A useful measure of the explanatory power of explanatory variables in an OLS regression is the goodness-of-fit statistic, the R^2. Because it is necessary to include the intercept term, which measures the time-varying aggregate return for the S&P/IFCI composite index, as an explanatory variable, we computed the R^2 that includes the explanatory power of the intercept term. By starting the regression analysis with the simplest model that includes only the intercept term, the aggregate return for the S&P/IFCI composite index, as an explanatory variable and then adding country factors or industry factors to the regression, it is possible to measure the increase in the R^2 that is associated with the inclusion of country or industry factors. This approach allows an inference to be made about the relative importance of country and industry factors in explaining cross-sectional variance in stock returns.

The results of this analysis are shown in Panel A and Panel B of **Figure 5.3**. Relatively low R^2s are obtained when only the IFCI emerging markets average return or industry sector effects are included in the regression. The explanatory power of the model increases sharply when the country effects are included in the regression. Thus, one may conclude that, consistent with our previous findings, country factors are dominant in explaining cross-sectional variance in emerging market stock returns.

Table 5.9. *F*-Test Country and Sector Regressions, 1 January 1990 through 1 January 2003

(number of times for each year that cross-sectional regressions reject the null hypothesis that country or industry has no effect on security returns)

	5 Percent Level of Significance				1 Percent Level of Significance			
	Equal Weighted		Value Weighted		Equal Weighted		Value Weighted	
Year	$\gamma = 0$	$\beta c = 0$	$\gamma = 0$	$\beta c = 0$	$\gamma = 0$	$\beta c = 0$	$\gamma = 0$	$\beta c = 0$
31 Country and 9 one-digit industry factors								
1990	2	12	8	12	1	12	7	12
1991	2	12	8	12	1	12	7	12
1992	2	12	8	12	1	12	7	12
1993	3	12	9	12	2	12	8	12
1994	3	12	9	12	2	12	8	12
1995	4	12	9	12	3	12	9	12
1996	3	12	9	12	2	12	8	12
1997	3	12	9	12	2	12	8	12
1998	4	12	9	12	3	12	8	12
1999	4	12	9	12	4	12	8	12
2000	4	12	9	12	4	12	8	12
2001	4	12	8	12	4	12	7	12
2002	5	12	9	12	5	12	8	12
31 Country and 63 two-digit industry factors								
1990	4	12	4	12	3	12	3	12
1991	4	12	4	12	3	12	3	12
1992	4	12	4	12	3	12	3	12
1993	4	12	4	12	3	12	3	12
1994	4	12	4	12	3	12	3	12
1995	4	12	4	12	2	12	2	12
1996	3	12	3	12	1	12	1	12
1997	3	12	3	12	1	12	1	12
1998	4	12	4	12	2	12	2	12
1999	5	12	5	12	3	12	3	12
2000	5	12	5	12	3	12	3	12
2001	6	12	6	12	3	12	3	12
2002	5	12	5	12	3	12	3	12

Note: See Appendix 2 for details.

Source: Based on data from S&P's EMDB.

Figure 5.3. Explanatory Power of Country and Industry Factors for Equal- and Value-Weighted Emerging Market Returns, December 1992–December 2002

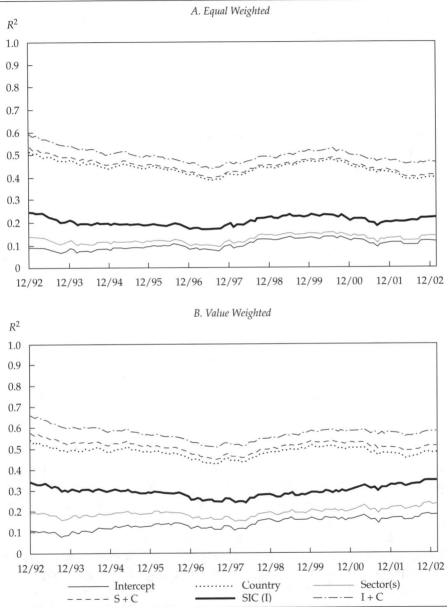

Note: Intercept = global factor; S + C = sector and country factors; SIC (I) = 63 two-digit industry factors; Sector (s) = nine one-digit sector factors; I + C = industry and country factors.

Source: Based on data from S&P's EMDB.

Currency Conversion and Country Effects

The empirical investigation described in this chapter reveals significant variation in intercountry emerging market returns. It also indicates that these variations are dominant factors in explaining cross-sectional variations among individual stocks in these markets. So far, however, this analysis does not offer an explanation about the economic drivers of the identified country factors. Likely candidates include institutional, legal, and financial infrastructure, as well as general economic policy.

In light of the recent currency crises in emerging markets, another probable driver of U.S. dollar returns for pure country portfolios is currency depreciation relative to the U.S. dollar. This hypothesis can be tested by running a regression of each of the pure country returns on the depreciation (or devaluation) of the local currency, defined as the monthly percent change in the exchange rate (as measured in local currency per U.S. dollar). **Table 5.10** reports the results. The R^2 regressions indicate that, on average, currency movements explain only a little more than 12 percent of the variance in pure country returns. But large cross-country variations are evident in the R^2s. Currency effects explain from 0.002 percent (Greece, value-weighted returns) to 43 percent (South Africa, equal-weighted returns) of the variance in pure country returns.

Conclusion

The results of our analysis strongly suggest that the country factor dominates in explaining individual securities returns in emerging markets. The industry factor appears to play a much less important role. These findings have three implications for practitioners.

First, for investors seeking diversification benefits, country diversification is more important than industry diversification.

Second, country specialists are important for institutional investors. Given the importance of the country factor, understanding the legal, institutional, and regulatory frameworks in a given country is important for valuing securities traded in that country. The ability to conduct meaningful country analysis is a vital skill for managers of emerging markets funds.

Third, an appropriate model for estimating the cost of capital in emerging markets should incorporate local market factors in addition to global ones. In light of these findings and the analysis in previous chapters, the next chapter examines how practitioners should modify the different methods recommended for valuing investments—and estimating the cost of capital—in emerging markets.

Table 5.10. Effect of Currency Devaluation on Emerging Market Returns, 1 January 1990 through 1 January 2003

(standard errors in parentheses)

Market	Equal-Weighted Monthly Return			Value-Weighted Monthly Return		
	Intercept	Depreciation Rate	R^2	Intercept	Depreciation Rate	R^2
Argentina	1.62%	−0.03%	0.17%	1.74%	−0.06%	0.63%
	(1.31)	(0.06)		(1.28)	(0.06)	
Brazil	3.31	−0.12	1.67	3.37	−0.12	1.59
	(1.55)*	(0.08)		(1.57)*	(0.08)	
Chile	2.09	−1.69	23.49	2.26	−1.68	23.82
	(0.57)***	(0.25)***		(0.55)***	(0.24)***	
China	0.66	−0.38	2.81	−0.03	−0.36	2.50
	(1.09)	(0.21)*		(1.09)	(0.21)*	
Colombia	2.15	−0.69	2.00	2.16	−0.68	1.97
	(1.10)*	(0.43)		(1.09)*	(0.43)	
Czech Republic	−0.40	−0.71	5.68	−0.13	−0.80	7.41
	(0.86)	(0.28)**		(0.84)	(0.27)***	
Egypt	−1.54	0.05	0.04	−1.71	0.19	0.40
	(0.73*)	(0.31)		(0.88)*	(0.37)	
Greece	1.23	0.04	0.11	1.24	0.01	0.00
	(0.92)	(0.11)		(0.88)	(0.10)	
Hungary	2.11	−0.22	0.17	1.77	−0.30	0.35
	(1.27)*	(0.50)		(1.15)	(0.46)	
India	1.23	−2.38	12.03	1.25	−2.31	13.98
	(0.80)	(0.59)***		(0.71)*	(0.52)***	
Indonesia	2.16	−1.02	37.39	1.31	−0.78	34.13
	(1.19)*	(0.11)***		(0.98)	(0.09)***	
Israel	1.39	−2.10	32.37	1.52	−1.85	30.90
	(0.86)	(0.36)***		(0.78)*	(0.33)***	
Jordan	0.97	−0.41	0.58	0.87	−0.55	1.28
	(0.42)*	(0.45)		(0.38)*	(0.41)	
Malaysia	1.60	−3.26	29.82	1.28	−2.46	29.56
	(0.97)*	(0.40)***		(0.74)*	(0.31)***	
Mexico	2.19	−1.19	35.45	2.49	−1.09	29.73
	(0.65)***	(0.13)***		(0.67)***	(0.13)***	
Morocco	0.15	−1.13	14.39	0.31	−1.04	13.66
	(0.63)	(0.33)***		(0.60)	(0.32)***	
Pakistan	2.11	−1.50	5.20	2.23	−1.38	4.62
	(1.22)*	(0.57)***		(1.20)*	(0.56)**	
Peru	1.61	−1.36	4.69	1.74	−1.42	5.91
	(0.89)*	(0.56)**		(0.82)*	(0.52)***	
Philippines	1.42	−2.45	28.55	0.62	−1.28	13.35
	(0.99)	(0.31)***		(0.83)	(0.26)***	

Table 5.10. Effect of Currency Devaluation on Emerging Market Returns, 1 January 1990 through 1 January 2003 (continued)

(standard errors in parentheses)

	Equal-Weighted Monthly Return			Value-Weighted Monthly Return		
Market	Intercept	Depreciation Rate	R^2	Intercept	Depreciation Rate	R^2
Poland	2.54%	0.11%	0.42	2.61%	0.11%	0.39
	(1.48)*	(0.16)		(1.49)*	(0.16)	
Portugal	0.77	−0.03	0.21	0.97	−0.07	1.00
	(0.62)	(0.06)		(0.64)	(0.06)	
Russia	3.31	−0.11	0.56	1.84	−0.17	1.59
	(2.80)	(0.18)		(2.61)	(0.17)	
Slovakia	−0.11	−0.55	1.87	−0.73	−0.97	9.69
	(1.40)	(0.54)		(1.05)	(0.40)**	
South Africa	2.22	−1.53	43.02	1.69	−1.32	42.54
	(0.66)***	(0.16)***		(0.57)***	(0.14)***	
South Korea	1.38	−1.64	32.40	1.30	−1.40	28.34
	(1.08)	(0.21)***		(1.01)	(0.20)***	
Sri Lanka	0.52	−0.69	0.75	0.76	−0.65	0.70
	(1.19)	(0.78)		(1.15)	(0.75)	
Taiwan, China	1.07	−2.69	14.78	1.12	−2.50	13.78
	(0.86)	(0.54)***		(0.83)	(0.52)***	
Thailand	0.88	−1.50	13.76	0.65	−1.24	13.19
	(1.11)	(0.30)***		(0.94)	(0.26)***	
Turkey	6.97	−1.04	11.83	6.41	−1.02	11.68
	(1.74)***	(0.23)***		(1.73)***	(0.23)***	
Venezuela	3.94	−0.52	9.38	3.96	−0.52	9.69
	(1.41)***	(0.14)***		(1.40)***	(0.14)***	
Zimbabwe	4.30	−1.16	30.60%	4.80	−1.13	32.37%
	(1.25)***	(0.18)***		(1.17)***	(0.17)***	

*Significant at the 10 percent level.
**Significant at the 2 percent level.
***Significant at the 1 percent level.
Source: Based on data from S&P's EMDB.

6. Valuation in Emerging Markets

The characteristics of emerging markets affect many of the typical valuation assumptions and thus require an adjustment in the methods used to value companies. This chapter first considers the different general valuation approaches that can be used, given that foreign currencies are involved. Finally, the focus shifts to a detailed examination of the steps investors should follow to complete the valuation of emerging market investments.

Basic Valuation Approaches

Two general discounted cash flow (DCF) valuation approaches are applicable for the valuation of an investment in a foreign market. If parity conditions hold, both methods should produce the same results, but each requires a different set of assumptions. **Figure 6.1** illustrates the two alternative approaches that can be used to derive a U.S. dollar net present value (NPV) from Mexican peso free cash flows.

- *Approach A.* The peso flows are converted to dollars, using the forecast of forward peso/dollar exchange rates. The dollar cash flows should be discounted using a dollar weighted-average cost of capital (WACC). Estimation of the dollar WACC must reflect not only the systematic risk of the target industry but also the local equity market and country risk (as described later in this chapter).[1] The end result is a DCF value denominated in dollars.

- *Approach B.* The local cash flows are discounted using a local WACC, resulting in a local NPV for the investment. Then, the local NPV is converted into a dollar NPV using the spot peso/dollar exchange rate.

Practitioners might argue at length about which approach is better. To focus the debate, it is useful to note that each approach has one or more embedded key bets, as well as various strengths and weaknesses, as summarized in **Exhibit 6.1**. The choice between the two depends on one's relative confidence in local capital market data versus one's relative confidence in the existence of a theoretical equilibrium in international currency and capital markets.

---

[1]Lessard (1996) gives an excellent presentation of the difference between these two types of risk and the need to adjust for both of them.

Figure 6.1. Two Approaches for Deriving a U.S. Dollar Net Present Value from Mexican Peso Free Cash Flows

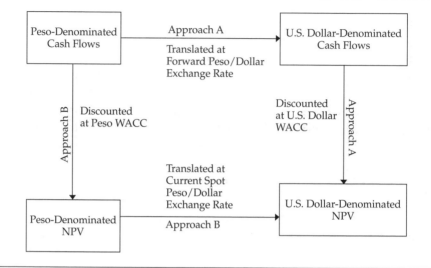

"Approach A" requires that future cash flows be converted from foreign to home currency before discounting them. Markets for most currencies rarely offer forward exchange rates beyond three years out. Because the valuation of most companies requires discounting future cash flows for a longer period, the investor must rely on exchange rate forecasts. Financial advisors and institutions routinely offer one- or two-year forecasts, but beyond this range, they offer only a qualitative outlook for the strength of one currency versus another. The only practical alternative on which the investor can rely is the interest rate parity formula (IRP).[2]

When used to translate foreign flows, however, the parity formula is subject to two assumptions worth examining critically. First, the investor should be confident about the inflation rate forecasts for home and foreign currencies. As a practical matter, forecasts of inflation beyond a year ahead are highly uncertain. This limitation means that the valuation analysis is

---

[2]IRP is a theoretical concept of equilibrium in international markets that precludes investors from arbitraging by taking advantage of different interest rates at local and foreign markets. As a result, fluctuations in exchange rates depend on the ratio of the local and foreign inflation rates. The academic consensus about IRP is that markets *tend toward* parity over time, although they virtually never achieve it. Macroeconomic shocks from commodity price changes (e.g., the oil embargo of 1974) and government policy changes are two possible causes of variance from parity.

Exhibit 6.1. Comparison of Two DCF Valuation Approaches Implied by Interest Rate Parity

Characteristic	Approach A	Approach B
Key features/ key bets	• PPP and IRP hold. • Inflation forecasts in pesos and dollars are appropriate. • Country risk premium estimate is appropriate.	• Local capital market has good availability and quality of data. • Local capital costs are free-market yields.
Strengths	• Theoretical rigor. • Can use (more reliable) capital market information from developed countries.	• Simplicity. • Translation at current spot rates.
Weaknesses	• PPP and IRP do not hold in all markets at all times. • Long-term forecasting of inflation is extremely difficult. • Implicitly assumes U.S. interest rates are consistent with forward peso/dollar exchange rates.	• Availability and quality of local capital market data. • Betas simply not available for many stocks in emerging markets. Investors must estimate their own betas. • Many interest rates are heavily administered by central banks and do not reasonably reflect inflation expectations or required real rates of return.

Note: Purchasing power parity (PPP) is a theoretical concept of equilibrium in international markets whereby a commodity costs the same across different currencies. In equilibrium, the exchange rate between two currencies should equal the ratio of commodity prices. The classic test of parity is the "Big Mac" index published semiannually by the *Economist* magazine—the routine finding is of a few sizable departures from parity and of broad but modest departure for most countries. Perhaps the academic consensus about PPP and IRP is that markets *tend toward* parity over time, although they virtually never actually achieve it. Macroeconomic shocks from commodity price changes (e.g., the oil embargo of 1974) and government policy changes are two possible causes of this.

heavily dependent on the practitioner's medium-term expectation of inflation in the home and foreign countries.

The second assumption is that parity prevails in global currency and capital markets. Research suggests that markets tend toward parity in the long run but deviation from parity in the short run is to be expected. Over the course of 10 or more years, parity may not be an unreasonable assumption. Over a shorter period, this assumption may be problematic. Thus, the investor's view of future short-term exchange rates can be incorporated into the valuation. On the other hand, "Approach B" requires the use of local market data to use a local discount rate. Therefore, the appropriateness of this approach depends on the investor's confidence in this data to estimate the local NPV. In deciding what approach to follow, the weaknesses of relying on local data should be compared with the weaknesses of the "Approach A" method.

Valuing Real versus Nominal Cash Flows

Given that inflation is a greater concern for developing countries than for traditional developed markets, investors will have the option of computing discounted cash flows based on nominal or real cash flows. When making the choice, the following points should be taken into consideration:

- *Value nominal cash flows at nominal discount rates.* Nominal cash flows are expected to grow at the compound product of the expected rate of inflation and the expected real rate of growth. Nominal discount rates are the compound product of the expected inflation rate and the expected real return. This "nominal/nominal" approach is the prevalent valuation method for global corporations.

- *Value real cash flows at real discount rates.* Real flows and rates reflect actual economic activity, apart from illusions created by aggregate price changes. One can think of this as the "zero inflation" approach. Practitioners in high-inflation environments use this "real/real" method for valuations in which the illusions become large.

In theory, if cash flows and discount rates are internally consistent, markets will value an asset the same way with either approach. Equality of results is obtained if the compounding and discounting are done at the same rate. The problem is that cash flows rarely compound at the same rate as the analyst's discount rate. For example, depreciation is usually a deductible expense for tax purposes, but in some countries, it is tied to the historical cost of the company's assets, not the current (inflation-adjusted) value. As inflation rises, companies will not deduct enough depreciation expense to replace assets as they age and investment outlays rise, thus resulting in the overpaying of taxes. In short, under the nominal cash flow/nominal discount rate approach, the distortion of historical-cost assets causes cash flows to be less than they would be with current-cost assets—an actual economic cost imposed on investors. The real/real approach ignores this distortion, unless the distortion is modeled explicitly. Some countries have ameliorated this distortion by permitting inflation indexing of asset values, in which case the real/real approach is more reasonable and, in theory, will yield valuation estimates similar to the nominal/nominal approach.

We encourage investors to research principles of inflation accounting in the emerging market. But in the absence of detailed information about accounting, the nominal/nominal approach best serves the goal of realistic estimates of value.

The Valuation Process

Ideally, investors should follow three separate steps in the valuation process. First, the investor must evaluate the general environment in which the investment will take place. A judgment about the environment will shape the way the valuation is performed. Second, the cash flows of the investment need to be forecast. Third, a decision has to be made regarding the cost of capital that will be used to discount those cash flows.

General Investment Environment. The general investment environment includes all the intangible attributes of a particular market that modify the risk of investing in it. In particular, investors should consider five key attributes—information environment, market integration, political risk, rule of law, and social issues.

- *Information environment.* The valuation of companies in any market relies on the availability of accurate and reliable information. The typical sources of information for foreign investors are accounting statements and the projections offered by financial analysts. These sources provide the foundation for judging the quality of the information environment in which a company operates. In Chapters 2 and 4, we concluded that emerging markets offer less information for investors and that, among emerging markets, wide differences exist in the availability and reliability of information. Thus, investors need to adapt to the information available for each market in which they invest.
- *Market integration.* The degree of local market integration with global markets is important because it affects one of the fundamental assumptions in valuation: that investors can engage in arbitrage, thereby driving returns toward a global equilibrium. If arbitrage is not possible, the reference point for investors will be the local, rather than global, cost of capital. Thus, integration affects the discount rate used for valuation in emerging markets. Approaches to estimating discount rates under segmentation and integration are discussed later in this chapter.
- *Political risk.* The extent to which local governments intervene in the working of markets and companies can have a material effect on the value of corporate assets. Such intervention occurs through means such as regulation, punitive tax policies, restrictions on cash transfers, and employment policies. Governments can intrude through outright expropriation of assets of foreign companies, or at the opposite extreme, governments can fail to protect when a breakdown in civil order occurs, as in insurrections and civil wars. Finally, official corruption, which is often a matter of tacit policy by local governments, is, in effect, an alternative form of taxation. Commercially available political risk measures show

wide variation among countries. The investor's view about the amount of political risk in a particular country will influence the estimation of cash flows, as well as the exchange rate.

- *Rule of law, corruption, corporate governance, and protection of minority shareholders.* The valuation of companies in any market depends on the degree to which investors' rights are protected. Share prices will be relatively lower if noncontrolling shareholders expect expropriation by either corrupt officials or controlling shareholders. Likewise, premiums for control will tend to be higher because controlling shareholders will probably have access to higher private rents. This situation is to be expected in emerging markets because they generally have a more corrupt environment than developed markets.

- *Social issues and culture.* Some business cultures endorse such practices as nepotism (employment of family members), paternalism (welfare-like support for employees' families), discrimination, charitable giving, tax evasion, official corruption, and reliance on government assistance. Investors should carefully consider the costs (perhaps hidden) imposed by these practices.

Analysts can adjust their valuation approach to account for the various attributes of emerging markets. The adjustments must be mutually exclusive so as to avoid double-counting. One can adjust cash flows downward, although this adjustment is typically arbitrary, or the discount rate upward using a measure of risk premium. The latter approach has the virtue of drawing on market rates for the adjustment and thus may be less arbitrary than the first approach.[3]

Estimating Cash Flows

Estimating the cash flows of an investment in an emerging market poses several considerations that are not typically encountered in a local developed market. The most important considerations are inflation, foreign currency exchange rates, tax rates, timing of remittance of cash, and accounting principles.

Inflation. Inflation rates for different countries vary widely. Simply applying the inflation rate of the United States, OECD (Organization for Economic

---

[3]Market rates are incorporated by comparing bond yields of two different markets. The difference between the yields is interpreted to be the premium that bondholders demand for assuming additional risk in the riskier market. To use this approach, both bonds must be denominated in the same currency (preferably dollars) and must be a similar class of asset (e.g., both must be sovereign bonds of the respective governments, or both must have the same corporate bond rating). Also, they should be "free market" yields, not subject to government intervention.

Cooperation and Development) countries, or the world economy to a particular country would be futile. Therefore, investors need to be explicit about their inflation assumptions for both cash flows and the discount rate. Above all, inflation assumptions should be handled consistently throughout the valuation analysis.

Foreign Currency Exchange Rates. Exchange rates between the foreign country and the investor's local country will presumably vary significantly during the life of the investment. Accordingly, in estimating cash flows, investors need to forecast exchange rate behavior for the life of the investment. For long-term investments, the use of IRP, coupled with inflation expectations, provides a rational method for estimating future exchange rate behavior, but this approach holds only if investors can move capital freely across borders. If, as in some emerging markets, such freedom does not exist, investors trying to establish expectations for exchange rates should consider capital controls and other macroeconomic policies that might prevent capital from flowing to the most profitable opportunities.

Tax Rates. The corporate tax rate affects both the forecasted cash flows and discount rate. As with inflation, being consistent throughout the valuation process is important. Marginal corporate tax rates vary substantially among countries, so using a single tax rate for investments in different countries would be inappropriate. In general, the investor should use a marginal tax rate appropriate to the country in which the cash flows are generated. This decision, however, will be affected by the tax system of the investor's country. For instance, the decision will vary depending on whether investors are exempt from taxation of foreign income.

Timing of Remittance of Cash. Investors should consider the possibility of not being able to move capital freely across borders. For example, some emerging markets are subject to limits in the outbound movement of cash and capital. Likewise, the timing of remittance of cash can affect taxation. For example, some countries, such as the United States, tax foreign income when it is received rather than earned. Thus, the timing of the return of cash to the investor should be explicitly modeled in the cash flow projections of an investment.

Accounting Principles. The process of deriving cash flows from financial statements requires familiarity with accounting principles in the foreign country. For example, in the United States, cash includes demand deposits and highly liquid investments; in New Zealand, short-term borrowing is deducted from the balance of cash. Mueller, Gernon, and Meek (1994) identify five distinct regional profiles of principles—Anglo-American-Dutch, Continental European, South American, mixed economy, and Islamic. Each system's particularities will affect the forecasting of cash flows, and analysts need to become familiar with them.

Estimating the Discount Rate

Asset-pricing theory, a subfield of financial economics that bears on investors' required rates of return, has amassed a body of research notable for its mathematical density, econometric complexity, numerous competing approaches and models, and spirited debate. This section offers but a few highlights and practical implications of asset-pricing theory (as well as directing interested readers to more detailed discussions). Note that in our discussion, "discount rate" refers to the WACC. Because the cost of debt, tax rate, and capital structure are relatively easily identified, the discussion related to the discount rate will focus on one component—the cost of equity.

As a general principle, investors should estimate a cost of equity consistent with the risk of the company in the emerging market. This principle steers the investor away from two classic errors—using a developed market discount rate for emerging market investments and using discount rates inappropriate for the target company's business risk. The venerable capital asset pricing model (CAPM) is perhaps the foundational expression of this principle. The following discussion explores the adaptation of CAPM to the emerging market setting.

An Overview of Models. Research offers numerous asset-pricing models that are potentially applicable to the emerging markets setting. Each model makes different assumptions about the pricing of securities and places differing demands on the practitioner for quality data and computational sophistication. **Exhibit 6.2** lists several models, divided according to two key attributes—quality of information and market segmentation/integration.

Investors need to address questions about information in three areas: market data, fundamental company information, and availability and quality of information. First, in terms of market data, can security prices be trusted to reflect what is known about companies? In other words, is the local market relatively efficient? Second, in regard to fundamental company information, is financial reporting transparent and reliable? Finally, concerning availability and quantity of information, is it possible to obtain prices or fundamental data in a long enough time series to establish trends using econometric techniques? Can a local market index dominated by one or two securities serve as an adequate proxy for the true market portfolio?

Exhibit 6.2. Applicability of Valuation Models According to Information and Integration in Local Markets

Information Environment	Target Country Integrated	Target Country Segmented
Foreign capital market information is easily obtained and believed to be reliable (e.g., the foreign capital market is relatively competitive and efficient, and financial performance reporting is relatively transparent and reliable).	• CAPM • Multifactor model	• Multifactor model • Credit model • CAPM adjusted for political risk and segmentation
Foreign capital market information is not easily obtained and/or is unreliable (e.g., the foreign capital market is relatively less competitive and inefficient, and/or financial performance reporting is relatively opaque and unreliable).	• CAPM	• CAPM adjusted for political risk and segmentation • Credit model

Chapter 2 and Chapter 4 suggest that the availability of high-quality information differs among markets. The following points can help the analyst form a judgment.

- *Market liquidity.* The prices observed in liquid markets can be assumed to be more reliable than those in illiquid markets. Because illiquid markets do not allow investors to shift their capital easily to attractive opportunities, perceived over- or undervaluations cannot be arbitraged rapidly.

- *Concentration ratios in market indexes.* A market index that is dominated by a few companies will reflect the performance of those companies, not necessarily the performance of the market as a whole.

- *Government intervention and regulation.* Governments can prevent prices from reflecting real market expectations through a variety of mechanisms. They can prevent capital movements, which leads to the same effects as those produced by a market's lack of liquidity. Also, they can actively intervene in the market as a large buyer or seller. In both of these circumstances, the resulting prices do not provide trustworthy information for forming investment expectations.

- *Market efficiency.* Prices might not reflect relevant information for making investment decisions. The conclusions of Chapter 4 clearly suggest that several emerging markets do not even display the weak form of market efficiency. In such circumstances, prices cannot be used to determine variables, such as expected returns and industry betas.

As with the case of information, beliefs about market segmentation call for different approaches to valuation. If a local market is integrated into the world market, its risk exposure will differ from that of a market segmented from the global market. One should consider different asset-pricing models according to the level of integration. Exhibit 6.2 depicts four general groups of models:

- *Where asset pricing is globally integrated and quality information may be obtained.* The northwest quadrant of the table perhaps characterizes large, multinational companies that are actively traded and listed for trading in developed country exchanges. These companies give financial reports to shareholders and disclose corporate news in ways consistent with developed country standards. One could logically assume that the securities of these companies are priced without segmentation. In this quadrant, one assumes that the investor has the capacity to estimate parameters for the models. Companies that operate in emerging markets that are on the "borderline" to become developed markets, such as South Korea, could fall in this quadrant, if the investor assumes they are integrated into the world market.

- *Where asset pricing is segmented and quality information may be obtained.* The northeast quadrant perhaps characterizes large companies actively traded in country exchanges for which the segmentation effects of emerging markets are expected. These companies, such as the large Brazilian oil company Petrobras, are well integrated into global product markets, followed by numerous securities analysts, and traded regularly in local markets, but their local equity markets may not be highly efficient, thus undermining investors' confidence that security prices reflect what is known.

- *Where asset pricing is globally integrated but foreign capital market information is questionable or difficult to obtain.* In the southwest quadrant, the investor chooses to make the assumption as if the target were globally integrated, even though the investor cannot obtain data believed to be reliable for econometric purposes. The models offered in this quadrant estimate required returns based on benchmarks from outside the emerging market and company. But it is worthwhile to ask whether one should assume the existence of a globally integrated market without reliable market data. The investor will probably find that such cases are exceptional.

- *Where asset pricing is segmented and information is questionable or difficult to obtain.* The southeast quadrant characterizes all new enterprises, joint ventures, project financings, and foreign direct investment in physical assets in segmented markets. Companies in emerging markets that are far from the possibility of being classified as developed (as discussed in Chapter 2) fall into this quadrant. The data problems are severe.

The main insight to draw from the variety of asset-pricing models is that one size does not fit all. Professional analysis of global investments begins with an understanding of the alternative models and the circumstances in which they are most likely to be useful.

There are five types of models—the CAPM, international CAPM, CAPM adjusted for political risk and segmentation, multifactor models, and the country credit model—that the investor can use when estimating a return rate in emerging markets. The choice depends on the investor's perception of the quality of the information environment and the segmentation between the emerging market and the investor's local market. For emerging markets that are integrated with global markets and for which quality information can be obtained, useful asset-pricing approaches include the CAPM, the international CAPM (ICAPM) and the multifactor model. On the other hand, the CAPM adjusted for political risk and segmentation is a useful approach when the investor considers that the market analyzed is not integrated with the home market. Finally, when quality information cannot be obtained, the credit model can be used.

CAPM. The point of departure is the familiar CAPM, which embodies the risk–return relationship fundamental to finance. The simplest starting point for asset pricing uses the home country risk-free rate and market premium with a beta appropriate for the target—for example, a beta selected from an average of company betas in the home country. Thus,

$$k_e = R_f + \beta_i \times (R_{Market} - R_f), \tag{1}$$

where

$$\beta_i = \frac{\sigma_{i,\,Market}}{\sigma^2_{Market}}$$

$\sigma_{i,\,Market}$ = covariance between the stock's returns and the home market returns

σ^2_{Market} = variance of home market

$R_{Market} - R_f$ = equity market risk premium

To estimate a discount rate appropriate for foreign cash flows, differences in inflation must be accounted for. One can use the concept of IRP to solve for foreign capital costs from home capital costs. Assuming constant real rates of return among countries, the ratio of the capital costs between two countries is equal to the ratio of the inflation rates between them. Rearranging these ratios yields this useful formula:

$$K_{Foreign} = \left[(1 + K_{Home}) \times \frac{\left(1 + Inf_{Foreign}\right)}{\left(1 + Inf_{Home}\right)} \right], \tag{2}$$

where

$K_{Foreign}$ = foreign cost of capital

K_{Home} = home cost of capital

$Inf_{Foreign}$ = foreign inflation rate

Inf_{Home} = home inflation rate

The classic CAPM would be appropriate for valuation across borders of two highly integrated country economies, such as the United States and Canada. For instance, a U.S. investor could use U.S.-based betas with the U.S. risk-free rate and equity premium to discount flows of Canadian dollars translated into U.S. dollars.

This approach is useful for analyzing companies in the southwest corner of Exhibit 6.2. It assumes away differences in political risk and capital market integration. The implicit assumption is that the difference between the results of a home CAPM and an ICAPM are negligible. This assumption allows the investor to use available international information and apply it in a particular country.

ICAPM. Several authors[4] have argued that, as the world becomes more integrated and more investors hold globally diversified portfolios, the relevant measure of a stock's risk is its covariance with the world market. Thus, the traditional CAPM model should be modified with substitute parameters that reflect risk and return in *world* markets. Accordingly, the formula for the ICAPM is:

$$k_e = R_f + \beta_i^w \times (R_m^w - R_f), \tag{3}$$

where

R_f = country risk-free rate

β_i^w = world beta of asset i

$R_m^w - R_f$ = world risk premium (in dollars)

The ICAPM assumes that markets are integrated and that reliable information can be obtained for feeding the model. Thus, ICAPM can be used for investments that fall in the northwest quadrant of Exhibit 6.2. Additionally, the ICAPM is relatively simple; it requires the same information that investors are used to looking for in the traditional CAPM, making it a typical choice when the particular circumstances of information and integration are met.

---

[4]For a discussion of ICAPM, see O'Brien (1999), Schramm and Wang (1999), and Stulz (1995, 1999).

CAPM Adjusted for Political Risk and Segmentation. Can CAPM be applied for valuation in emerging markets where these markets are not integrated? Yes, it can, with adjustments. Lessard (1996) argued that a U.S. company's beta for an investment in an offshore project would be the product of a beta for the project (as if domestic) and a "country beta" reflecting the volatility of the U.S. equity market relative to the volatility of the offshore equity market:

$$\beta_{Offshore\ project} = \beta_{U.S.\ project} \times \beta_{Offshore\ equities\ vs.\ U.S.\ equities} \tag{4}$$

For example, the country beta of the Argentine equity market relative to the United States is estimated as:

$$\beta_{Argentina\ vs.\ United\ States} = \rho_{Argentina/United\ States} \times \frac{\sigma_{Argentina}}{\sigma_{Unites\ States}} \tag{5}$$

where ρ is the correlation in returns between Argentina and U.S. equities and σ measures standard deviations of equity returns in the two markets. In 1996, the country betas of the Argentine, Brazilian, and Chilean equity markets versus the United States were 1.96, 2.42, and 0.65, respectively, as shown in **Table 6.1.**[5]

Table 6.1. Example Country Betas and Their Components

Country	Country Beta	Local Volatility	U.S. Volatility	Correlation (local with U.S.)
Argentina	1.96	61.93%	10.08%	0.32
Brazil	2.42	60.86	10.08	0.40
Chile	0.65	28.54%	10.08%	0.23

Lessard (1996) described the country risk premium method. This method adjusts the CAPM to account for segmentation and political risk:[6]

$$K_e = R_f^{U.S.} + \pi + (\beta_i^{U.S.} \times \beta^{Country}) \times (R_{Market}^{U.S.} - R_f^{U.S.}) \tag{6}$$

where

π = country credit spread, measured by yield differentials between U.S. government bonds and U.S. dollar-denominated sovereign bonds of the same tenor

---

[5]To estimate these betas, we used data provided by the International Finance Corporation. See *Emerging Stock Markets Factbook* (1996).

[6]Lessard suggested that other sources of overseas investment risk, such as those of operating risk, demand risk, and domestic market price risk, among others, may be modeled directly into the cash flows.

$\beta_i^{U.S.}$ = domestic beta of asset i in the United States

$\beta^{Country}$ = beta of domestic market versus U.S. market

Because the country credit spread is calculated directly from yields on dollar-denominated bonds rather than from local currency bonds, it does not incorporate any currency effects.[7] What results is a sovereign risk-free rate denominated in U.S. dollars.

In contrast with Lessard's model, other analysts believe that such risks are better incorporated into cash flows rather than a discount rate. Some risks are reduced over time through experience or hedging and insurance contracts. In such cases, capturing the relevant risk in the discount rate would not be appropriate because doing so would not reflect the declining nature of the risk.

Also, the cross-product of the two betas has a troublesome mathematical property. Bodnar, Dumas, and Marston (2002) have shown that this adjusted CAPM violates assumptions of linearity, which makes the results less reliable in a statistical sense and more difficult to interpret.

The fact that local prices will be determined increasingly by "global" investors presents a dilemma for local investors who are unable to diversify internationally. Because their portfolios are restricted to the domestic market, theory would dictate that they use the local CAPM method to determine costs of equity. By virtue of measuring beta against the domestic market, however, they may come up with higher costs of equity than would a "global" investor.

Multifactor Model. Various researchers argued that the risks in international investing are not adequately modeled by the ICAPM model and thus have suggested using more fully specified econometric models.[8] Under this approach, the required return on a security is equal to a risk-free rate plus the exposure of the stock to various factors, which could be macroeconomic factors (such as economic growth, inflation, and consumer confidence) or company factors (such as size, leverage, and earnings volatility):

$$k_e = R_f + \beta_1 \times RP_1 + \beta_2 \times RP_2 + \cdots + \beta_k \times RP_k. \tag{7}$$

The main advantage of multifactor models is the explicit inclusion of different factors that can affect the required rate of return requested by investors. As a result, multifactor models display higher explanatory power than other models. Furthermore, because one of these factors can be integration,

---

[7]Lessard argued that currency effects may have a significant impact on cash flows but not on market covariance risk. Of currency risks, he wrote that "since they are the relative prices of different currencies, by definition they cannot affect all assets in the same way." As such, they do not require a premium.

[8]For example, see Bodnar, Dumas, and Marston (2002); Errunza and Losq (1985, 1987); Solnik (1976, 1996); Diermeier and Solnik (2001); and Cavaglia, Hodrick, Vadim, and Zhang (2002).

the multifactor model can be used regardless of the assumption about how integrated a particular market is. On the other hand, multifactor models require a great amount of data and computational analysis. They also require including the right factors but do not suggest which ones they should be. Finally, the information that feeds the models must be reliable (or at least systematically unreliable) in order for investors to have confidence in the output. By definition, this final condition is not met in markets where reliable data cannot be found, and its use is not recommended for those markets.

Credit Model. Whereas the previous methods assume that reliable data can be found, the credit model relaxes this assumption and tries to substitute for lack of information (although it can also be used with reliable information). For instance, given market imperfections, beta may have little meaning in an emerging market setting, and some local market settings simply may not have a stock market. Erb, Harvey, and Viskanta (1995) offered a model based on the country credit risk rating:

$$K_{i,t+1} = \gamma_0 + \gamma_1 \times \ln(\text{Country Credit Risk Rating}_{it}) + \varepsilon_{it+1}. \tag{8}$$

By relying on nonequity market measures, the model can circumvent estimation difficulties related to the lack of market information. Also, measures of country risk impound assessments of political, currency, segmentation, and other types of risks to which an enterprise might be subject. Furthermore, estimates of cost of capital may be obtained from public sources and do not require a large volume of data analysis.[9] Because this model estimates an average required equity return for a country, however, adjusting the estimate for company-specific risk is necessary. This model is valuable in the most precarious circumstances of information availability.

Does the Choice of Model Matter?

The range of models invites the question of whether the resulting estimates differ by much. **Exhibit 6.3** summarizes the differences among the models and suggests considerations for selecting which model to use. For investments among developed countries, the difference in choice of model may be less significant, but between developed and emerging markets, the choice of model makes a sizable difference. Bruner and Chan (2002) estimated the effects of choosing different methods by focusing on five markets classified by the World Bank as "emerging"—Brazil, South Africa, Thailand, Malaysia,

---

[9]One of the coauthors of the credit model, Professor Campbell Harvey, makes the estimation program available for purchase. See www.duke.edu/~charvey/applets/iccrc.html.

Exhibit 6.3. Summary of Comparison of Cost of Equity Models

Model	Advantages	Other Considerations
ICAPM • Usually estimated in a *numeraire* currency, such as the dollar or euro.	• Expression of integrated world markets. • Permits comparison of all equities against a common benchmark, the global equity market portfolio. • Simple model.	• Supposes no segmentation or home bias. • Betas for ICAPM generally must be estimated by the analyst. • Requires data and computational skill. • Offers relatively low explanatory power (R^2).
Multifactor model • Usually estimated in a *numeraire* currency, such as the dollar or euro.	• Most flexible model. Permits inclusion of any suspected sources of risk. • Probably highest explanatory power of any class of model.	• Coefficients must be estimated by the analyst. Requires data and computational skill. • Theory does not dictate which factors should be included in the model.
CAPM • Can be estimated in home currency (adjusted for industry beta only). • Can be estimated in foreign currency (adjusted for beta and inflation).	• Simple application of typical domestic model. • Allows estimate of discount rate in foreign currency without relying on foreign data.	• Supposes no segmentation or home bias. • Requires a "view" about expected inflation in home and foreign currencies.
Local CAPM • Estimated in foreign currency. • Can be translated to home currency through inflation adjustment model.	• Simple extension of typical domestic model. • Enables assessment of segmentation.	• Relies on trustworthy local capital market data. • Analyst may need to estimate beta. Requires data and computational skill.
Adjusted CAPM • Estimated in home currency (as presented in text).	• Transparency: enables assessment of segmentation and political risk.	• Returns may not be linear in cross-product of country and company betas. • Requires country beta, which may need to be estimated by the analyst. • Requires country risk premium, which may require analyst judgment.
Credit model • Usually estimated in a *numeraire* currency, such as the dollar or euro.	• Intuitively appealing focus on country; permits assessment of segmentation. • Based on analyst estimates of country risk. • Lower requirement for data. • Coefficients are commercially available.	• Gives cost of equity estimates for equity market index of a country. Must be adjusted further for company-specific risks.

and Poland. They selected two of the five largest companies in terms of market cap and estimated costs of equity for each company using, among others, the following methods:

- CAPM,
- CAPM adjusted for political risk and segmentation,
- ICAPM,
- multifactor method.

Although in some cases they found similar costs of capital for different models, in general, the authors found material differences in estimates generated by them—on the order of 300 to 1,000 bps. They attributed these differences to alternative beta estimates, inflation, political risk, and equity market returns. The bottom line seems to be that the cost of equity differences are large among emerging economies and among models. When valuing assets in emerging markets, one must have a view about estimation of discount rates.

Summary

To conduct a valuation in an emerging market, investors can draw on at least two currency translation strategies, two approaches to incorporating inflation, and many models for discount rate estimation. To illustrate how the choices might be combined, we offer the following advice for valuation of an emerging market investment.

- *Use DCF.* The DCF model, practiced rigorously, is the only approach that affords the investor any comparability among investment opportunities in countries as diverse as Germany, Argentina, and Mali.
- *Estimate cash flows of the analyzed company in its local currency.* This approach is the best way to capture local tax and inflation effects.
- *Translate those local cash flows to home currency at forward exchange rates as estimated from the IRP formula:*

$$FWD_{Peso/Dollar} = Spot_{Peso/Dollar} \left[\frac{(1 + Inf_{Peso})}{(1 + Inf_{Dollar})} \right]. \tag{9}$$

To use this formula, the investor needs a view about the long-term inflation rates in the foreign and home currencies.

- *Discount local cash flows at a rate consistent with a local-currency-based estimate of foreign country inflation, country political risk, country beta, and industry beta.*

7. Conclusion

Emerging markets differ from developed markets and from each other in important ways. In general, they are not as large, liquid, or transparent as developed markets. The accounting, governance, and legal "rules" by which they operate vary widely, and their return performance is not closely linked with the performance of other markets with which investors may be familiar. To invest in emerging markets, portfolio managers need to accommodate departures from traditional investment practices and frameworks.

Historically, emerging markets have offered high rates of return and high risk (or volatility), along with low return correlations with developed markets. Thus, in theory, passively including emerging markets equities in portfolios could give investors higher returns and a reasonable level of risk because of the low correlations. As we have explained in this monograph, however, the correlation of emerging markets with developed markets has increased over time, making the low-correlation argument for including emerging markets less attractive. In light of this fact, a better way to think of emerging markets is in the context of risk and return for developed and emerging markets. Emerging markets do offer higher risk, but since 1999, overall market volatility in developed markets has increased and their expected returns have decreased substantially. Consequently, the growth potential and resulting potential returns of emerging markets may now offer an attractive risk–return trade-off relative to developed markets. This perspective necessarily shifts the discussion away from a focus on returns and toward risk tolerance. In this context, the decision to include emerging markets in an institutional portfolio depends on the level of risk tolerance. Institutional investors that include venture capital and hedge funds in their portfolios could view emerging markets as attractive. Funds that avoid these types of investments would find emerging markets less attractive.

Once a decision is made to invest in emerging markets, the key issues are where and how. Deciding where to invest requires a discussion of whether industry sectors or countries determine the overall returns in emerging markets. We find strong evidence that country factors dominate industry sectors in emerging markets. For institutional investors, this finding means that country diversification is more important than sector diversification. Focusing on countries matters. Unlike developed markets, for which economic policy tools are usually applied with consistency over time, emerging market countries have less consistency in policy issues. Even when they commit to a consistent policy, they have less control over their environment and are often subject to substantial shocks that can easily overwhelm domestic policy. Hence, it is important to identify the factors (such as liquidity, information availability, market efficiency, and corruption) that can have an effect at the country level.

Because countries should be the main focus of investing in emerging markets, our analysis throughout the monograph argues strongly for active management. The wide variation between countries in terms of liquidity, information, market efficiency, and corruption makes a strong case for active management. These risk factors often are not efficiently reflected in investors' calculations of expected returns, and incorporating them into such calculations represents an opportunity for managers to enhance performance through active management.

In addition to actively managing country selection, investment managers face the decision of whether to hedge currency risk. Our analysis of the effects of currency on country returns does support hedging currency risk, but the support is not overwhelming. In general, one would expect an emerging market's currency to appreciate in real terms in the long run, as the country develops and experiences faster productivity growth. In addition, currency appreciation in real terms in an emerging market country would be expected to be positively correlated with the excess return of the securities in that market (i.e., as benchmarked against returns of securities in developed markets). Thus, hedging should help reduce both the volatility and expected returns of emerging market securities.

Once an investor decides on country selection and currency hedging, an important issue is how the active management gets implemented at the level of the individual company. Our examination of market efficiency in emerging markets shows scant evidence that these markets are efficient at the company level. This finding has strong implications for how investors might go about deciding to invest in individual companies within a country. The typical distinction is between a quantitative and fundamental approach. Most quantitative approaches focus on finding key attributes or factors that help identify undervalued stocks. A key assumption is that these factors are stable over time. Given the basic instability we found in emerging markets, however, little value is likely to be added through a quantitative approach to stock selection in these markets. A fundamental approach seems to offer more potential value. The market inefficiencies at the company level should offer the opportunity to profit from information.

Two overarching themes concern the analysis of emerging markets in this monograph. First, analysts and portfolio managers need to decide whether the information they can find in an emerging market is reliable enough and available in sufficient quantity to use in the country and company evaluation process. Second, analysts need to have a view about whether the emerging market in which they are considering investing is integrated, or in the process of becoming integrated with, global markets. The answers to these questions are the key to choosing the appropriate investment approach and valuation method to be used in dealing with emerging markets.

Answering these questions requires significant research. This fact, combined with the apparent segmentation that continues among emerging markets, suggests that the use of country specialists will likely be an ongoing requirement for investing in emerging markets.

Appendix A. Estimating the Total Risk Attributed to the Overall Market Movements

Determining the risk of a particular stock attributed to overall market movements is relevant in making an assumption about the amount of company-specific information in the market. This appendix describes the mechanism for measuring such risk.

Borrowing from the CAPM framework, the return on a particular stock can be written as follows:

$$R_{i,t} = R_f + \beta_i \times (R_{m,t} - R_f) + e_{i,t},$$

where

$R_{i,t}$ = the return on a stock for time t

R_f = the risk-free rate of return

β_i = the beta of stock i

$R_{m,t}$ = the return on the market portfolio for time t

$\varepsilon_{i,t}$ = the error term that captures the impact of company-specific information

Estimating the total variance of $R_{i,t}$ yields

$$\sigma^2(R_i) = \beta_i^2 \times \sigma^2(R_m) + \sigma^2(e_i).$$

In this formulation, the total variability of a stock can be broken into two parts: the market portion, $\beta_i^2 \times \sigma^2(R_m)$, and a company-specific portion, $\sigma^2(e_i)$. In the estimate $\phi = [\beta_i^2 \times \sigma^2(R_m)]/\sigma^2(R_i)$, ϕ is the portion of total risk attributed to the overall market movements and $(1 - \phi)$ is the proportion of total risk attributable to the impact of company-specific information. Therefore, ϕ can be used as a proxy for company-specific information. Low values of ϕ for companies in a particular market should infer more company-specific information.

To estimate ϕ for a set of emerging markets, we used monthly data on individual company returns from the emerging market database for the period from January 1995 through December 2002. Next, using all of the companies available in a particular market, we calculated an equal-weighted return for each market, which we used to run an OLS regression for each company. The time-series return for a particular stock was regressed against the relevant market return. Finally, we calculated the average R^2 of the regressions for each market. In this context, the R^2 would be ϕ. Table 4.2 reports the market monthly standard deviation of return for each market and the mean ϕ, the proportion of an individual company's total risk attributable to market movements in the company's home market. Table 4.2 also reports the same statistics for a sample of stocks listed on the NYSE for the same period.

Appendix B. Country versus Industry Regression Model

This appendix shows in more detail how we estimated the relative importance of country and industry factors in explaining individual stock performance in emerging markets. The model follows the method used in Heston and Rouwenhorst (1994).

The Model

To begin the analysis, consider the null hypothesis that country and industry factors are insignificant in explaining stock returns in emerging markets. Under this hypothesis, the return on the nth security in the universe of IFCI emerging market countries, R_{nt}, can be decomposed into two parts:

$$R_{nt} = \alpha_t + \varepsilon_{nt}, \tag{B1}$$

where α_t is a time-varying return on the aggregate S&P/IFCI composite index and ε_{nt} is an idiosyncratic component assumed to have mean zero and finite variance. The return on the equal-weighted S&P/IFCI composite index can then be estimated as

$$\hat{\alpha}_t^e = \frac{1}{N} \sum_{n-1}^{N_t} R_{nt}, \tag{B2}$$

and the return on the value-weighted S&P/IFCI composite index can be estimated as

$$\hat{\alpha}_t^v = \frac{1}{N} \sum_{n-1}^{N_t} w_{nt} R_{nt}, \tag{B3}$$

where N_t is the number of securities included in the universe of S&P/IFCI stocks in period t, and w_{nt} is company n's share of investable market cap in emerging markets at time t, $\sum_{n=1}^{N_t} w_{nt} = 1$. Figure 5.1 plots the 36-month moving average of the equal-weighted and value-weighted returns of the S&P/IFCI Composite Index. It shows the significant impact of emerging market crises in the late 1990s on returns. Consistent with Table 5.1, Figure 5.1 also shows that value-weighted returns are, on average, lower than equal-weighted returns but have less volatility.

Given the observed variations in the average returns for emerging markets countries and sectors, as shown in Table 5.1, country and industry factors would be expected to have some power in explaining the variation in company returns. Under the alternative hypotheses that country and industry factors are individually or jointly significant determinants of returns, a better specification for decomposing R_{nt}, the return on the nth security that belongs to country c and industry i, can be written as

$$R_{nt} = \alpha_t + \beta_{ct} + \gamma_{it} + \varepsilon'_{nt}, \tag{B4}$$

where α_t again measures the time-varying return on the IFCI Composite Index; the time-varying country-specific effect, β_{ct}, measures the incremental contribution to firm n's return arising from the company's exposure to risks that are unique in its home country c; and the time-varying industry effect, γ_{it}, is the incremental contribution to company n's return arising from the firm's exposure to risks that are unique in industry i; and ε'_{nt} measures the idiosyncratic component of the return on security n, which by construction is orthogonal to country and industry effects, has zero mean, and is assumed to have finite variance.

With the available data, this model allows for a total of 31 country effects, one for each country in the sample. Depending on industry classification, the model allows for either a total of 9 one-digit industry effects or a total of 63 two-digit industry effects. This specification assumes that a security has exposure to its own country and industry but no exposure to other countries and sectors. In addition, it assumes that the country and industry factors have separate influences on returns, and therefore no interaction terms between country and industry as explanatory variables.

By aggregating the common return on each security to α_t, the aggregate average country or industry effect is set to equal zero. Thus, α_t is defined as the benchmark return on the IFCI Composite Index and β_{ct} and γ_{it} measure how each country c and each industry i differ from the IFCI benchmark. The country and industry effects are thus measured relative to the IFCI equal-weighted (or value-weighted) market. For country c, β_{ct} is therefore a measure of the pure excess return on the country portfolio in period t, obtained after removing identified industry effects. Similarly, for industry i, γ_{it} measures the pure excess return on the industry portfolio in period t, obtained after removing identified country effects.

To implement this definition and estimate the equal-weighted country and industry effects, the following restrictions are imposed for each period t:

$$\sum_{n=1}^{N_t} \beta_{ct} = \sum_{c=1}^{C} N_{ct} \beta_{ct} = 0 \tag{B5}$$

and

$$\sum_{n=1}^{N_t} \gamma_{it} = \sum_{i=1}^{I} M_{it} \gamma_{it} = 0, \tag{B6}$$

where C and I are the total number of countries and industries in the sample, and N_{ct} and M_{it} are the number of securities in country c and industry i in period t. Under these restrictions, the equal-weighted IFCI benchmark return can still be estimated using Equation A2. But to jointly estimate α_t, β_{ct} for each country and γ_{it} for each industry, the specified linear model is rewritten as

$$R_{nt} = \alpha_t + \sum_{c=1}^{C} \beta_{ct} D_{nc}^C + \sum_{i=1}^{I} \gamma_{it} D_{ni}^I + \varepsilon'_{nt}, \tag{B7}$$

where D_{nc}^c denotes a country dummy variable that equals 1 if firm n belongs to country c and zero otherwise and D_{ni}^I denotes a sector dummy variable that equals 1 if firm n belongs to industry i and zero otherwise. An ordinary least-squares (OLS) regression is run on Equation A7 at each period t subject to the constraints in Equation A5 and Equation A6 using cross-sectional data. Thus, time-varying equal-weighted estimates $\hat{\alpha}_t^e$, $\hat{\beta}_{ct}^e$, and $\hat{\gamma}_{st}^e$ are obtained.

Given our definition and empirical implementation, $\hat{\alpha}_t^e$ is the OLS estimate of the return on the equal-weighted IFCI Composite Index in each period t, which is identical to the estimate obtained by aggregating individual security returns using Equation A2. Our definition and empirical implementation also imply that $\hat{\alpha}_t^e + \hat{\beta}_{ct}^e$ measures the equal-weighted pure country return on an industrially diversified portfolio of companies in country c that is free of the industry effects identified by the regression model (Equation A7). As in Heston and Rouwenhorst, an industrially diversified portfolio in this context is a portfolio that has the same industry composition as the IFCI equal-weighted emerging markets index. Similarly, $\hat{\alpha}_t^e + \hat{\gamma}_{it}^e$ is an estimate of the pure return on the industry portfolio i that is free of the country effects identified by the regression model (Equation A7). This industry portfolio is geographically diversified so as to have the same country composition as the IFCI equal-weighted emerging markets index.

The regression analysis can also be used to obtain value-weighted returns on pure country portfolios and pure industry portfolios by estimating Equation A7 using weighted OLS. The weights are simply the investable market cap of the securities at the beginning of the month. The restrictions that imply that the value-weighted IFCI index returns α_t^v are free from country and industry effects become

$$\sum_{c=1}^{C} w_{ct}\beta_{ct} = 0 \tag{B8}$$

and

$$\sum_{t=1}^{I} v_{it}\gamma_{it} = 0, \tag{B9}$$

where w_{ct} and v_{it} are the value weights of country c and industry i in the IFCI value-weighted emerging markets index, $\sum_c w_{ct} = 1$, and $\sum_i v_{it} = 1$. Under these restrictions, the weighted OLS estimate of the regression intercept, $\hat{\alpha}_t^v$, is the return on the IFCI value-weighted emerging markets index, and the weighted OLS estimates $\hat{\alpha}_t^v + \hat{\beta}_{ct}^v$ and $\hat{\alpha}_t^v + \hat{\gamma}_{it}^v$ measure the returns on the value-weighted pure country c portfolio and pure industry i portfolio.

To observe the statistical significance of the results obtained, F-tests were conducted on the results obtained using 31 country effects and 9 sector effects. The null hypothesis for testing the joint significance of the 31 country effects at any period t is

$$\beta_{ct} = 0 \text{ for } c = 1, \ldots, 31, \tag{B10}$$

and the null hypothesis for testing the joint significance of either 9 one-digit industry effects or 63 two-digit industry effects is

$$\gamma_{it} = 0 \text{ for } i = 1, \ldots, 9 \text{ or } I = 1, \ldots, 63. \tag{B11}$$

The alternative hypotheses are (1) that at least one of the country effects and (2) at least one of the industry effects are different from zero. We performed tests using cross-sectional data in each month. Table 5.9 reports the number of times (out of a total of 12) in each year that each of the null hypotheses was rejected by the data.

The results obtained through the use of this model are discussed in Chapter 5.

References

Abeysekera, Sarath P. 2001. "Efficient Markets Hypothesis and the Emerging Capital Market in Sri Lanka: Evidence From the Colombo Stock Exchange—A Note." *Journal of Business, Finance and Accounting*, vol. 28, nos. 1/2:249–261.

Antoniou, A., N. Ergul, P. Holmes, and R. Priestly. 1997. "Technical Analysis, Trading Volume and Market Efficiency: Evidence From an Emerging Market." *Applied Financial Economics*, vol. 7, no. 4 (August):361–365.

Bekaert, G., and C. Harvey. 1997. "Emerging Equity Market Volatility." *Journal of Financial Economics*, vol. 43, no. 1 (January):29–77.

Bekaert, G., C. Harvey, and A. Ng. Forthcoming 2003. "Market Integration and Contagion." *Journal of Business*.

Bekaert, G., C. Erb, C. Harvey, and T. Viskanta. 1997. "What Matters for Emerging Equity Market Investments," *Emerging Markets Quarterly*, vol. 1, no. 1 (Summer):14–19.

Bodnar, G., B. Dumas, and R. Marston. 2002. "Cross-Border Valuation: The International Cost of Capital." Working paper, INSEAD.

Bohm, Norberto, Robert F. Bruner, Susan Chaplinsky, Caio Costa, Miguel Fernandez, Pablo Manriquez, and Joaquin Rodriguez-Torres. 2000. "Practices of Private Equity Firms in Latin America." Darden Case Collection, Darden Graduate School of Business Administration, University of Virginia.

Bruner, R., and J. Chan. 2002. "The Risk Premium for Investing in Emerging Markets: What Is It? Where Is It?" Working paper, Darden Graduate School of Business Administration, University of Virginia.

Bruner, Robert F., Robert M. Conroy, and Wei Li. 2002. "Valuation in Emerging Markets." CD-ROM, Darden Case Collection, Darden Graduate School of Business Administration, University of Virginia.

Bruner, R., K. Eades, R. Harris, and R. Higgins. 1998. "'Best Practices' in Estimating the Cost of Capital: Survey and Synthesis." *Journal of Financial Practice and Education* (Spring/Summer):13–28.

Cavaglia, S., R. Hodrick, M. Vadim, X. Zhang. 2002. "Pricing the Global Industry Portfolios." National Bureau of Economic Research, Working Paper 9344.

Cheung, Yan-Leung, Kei-Ann Wong, and Yan-ki Ho. 1993. "The Pricing of Risky Assets in Two Emerging Asian Markets—Korea and Taiwan." *Applied Financial Economics*, vol. 3, no. 4:315–324.

Demirer, Riza, and M. Baha Karan. 2002. "An Investigation of the Day-of-the-Week Effect on Stock Returns in Turkey." *Emerging Markets, Finance and Trade*, vol. 38, no. 6 (November/December):47–77.

Diermeier, J., and B. Solnik. 2001. "Global Pricing of Equity." *Financial Analysts Journal*, vol. 57, no. 4 (July/August):37–47.

Durnev, Artyom, Randall Morck, Bernard Yeung, and Paul Zarowin. 2001. "Does Greater Firm-Specific Return Variation Mean More or Less Informed Stock Pricing?" Working paper, University of Alberta.

Erb, Claude, Campbell R. Harvey, and Tadas E. Viskanta. 1995. "Country Risk and Global Equity Selection." *Journal of Portfolio Management*, vol. 21, no. 2 (Winter):74–83.

Errunza, V., and E. Losq. 1985. "International Asset Pricing under Mild Segmentation: Theory and Test." *Journal of Finance*, vol. 40, no. 1 (March):105–124.

———. 1987. "How Risky Are Emerging Markets?" *Journal of Portfolio Management*, vol. 14, no. 1 (Fall):62–68.

Estrada, Javier. 2002. "Systematic Risk in Emerging Markets: The D-CAPM." *Emerging Markets Review*, vol. 3, no. 4 (December):365–379.

Forbes, K., and R. Rigobon. 2002. "No Contagion, Only Interdependence: Measuring Stock Market Co-Movements." *Journal of Finance*, vol. 57, no. 5 (October):2223–61.

Godfrey, Stephen, and Ramon Espinosa. 1996. "A Practical Approach to Calculating Costs of Equity for Investments in Emerging Markets." *Journal of Applied Corporate Finance*, vol. 9, no. 5 (Fall):80–89.

Gordan, Barry, and Libby Rittenberg. 1995. "The Warsaw Stock Exchange: A Test of Market Efficiency." *Comparative Economic Studies*, vol. 37, no. 2:1–27.

Graham, J., and C. Harvey. 2001. "The Theory and Practice of Corporate Finance: Evidence From the Field." *Journal of Financial Economics*, vol. 60, nos. 2/3 (May/June):187–243.

Harvey, C. 1995. "Predictable Risk and Returns in Emerging Markets." *Review of Financial Studies*, 8:773–816.

Heston, Steven, and Geert Rouwenhorst. 1994. "Does Industrial Structure Explain the Benefits of International Diversification?" *Journal of Financial Economics*, vol. 36, no. 1:3–27.

Huang, Bwo-Nung. 1995. "Do Asian Stock Market Prices Follow Random Walks? Evidence From the Variance Ratio Test." *Applied Financial Economics*, vol. 5, no. 2:251–256.

International Finance Corporation. 1998. *Emerging Stock Markets Factbook 1999*. Washington, DC.

Jha, Raghbendra, and Hari K. Nagarajan. 2000. "The Structure and Price Efficiency of an Emerging Market." *International Journal of Commerce and Management*, vol. 10, no. 2:50–59.

Kritzman, K., and S. Page. 2003. "The Hierarchy of Investment Choice: A Normative Interpretation." *Journal of Portfolio Management*, vol. 29, no. 4 (Summer):11–24.

Lamba, Asjeet, and Isaac Otchere. 2001. "An Analysis of the Dynamic Relationships between the South African Equity Market and Major World Equity Markets." *Multinational Finance Journal*, vol. 5, no. 3:201–224.

Laurence, Martin, Francis Cai, and Sun Qian. 1997. "Weak-Form Efficiency and Causality Tests in Chinese Stock Markets." *Multinational Finance Journal*, vol. 1, no. 4:291–307.

Lessard, Donald R. 1996. "Incorporating Country Risk in the Valuation of Offshore Projects." *Journal of Applied Corporate Finance*, vol. 9, no. 3 (Fall):52–63.

Long, D. Michael, Janet D. Payne, and Chenyang Feng. 1999. "Information Transmission in the Shanghai Equity Market." *Journal of Financial Research*, vol. 22, no. 1:29–45.

Morck, Randall, Bernard Yueng, and Wayne Yu. 2000. "The Information Content of Stock Markets: Why Do Emerging Markets Have Synchronous Stock Price Movements?" *Journal of Financial Economics*, vol. 58, nos. 1/2:215–260.

Mueller, G., H. Gernon, and G. Meek. 1994. *Accounting: An International Perspective*. 3rd ed. Burr Ridge, IL: McGraw-Hill/Irwin.

O'Brien, T. 1999. "The Global CAPM and A Firm's Cost of Capital in Different Currencies." *Journal of Applied Corporate Finance*, vol. 12, no. 3 (Fall):73–79.

Ojah, Kalu, and David Karemera. 1999. "Random Walks and Market Efficiency Test of Latin American Emerging Equity Markets: A Revisit." *The Financial Review*, vol. 34, no. 2:57–72.

Pereiro, Luis. 2002. "Valuing Companies in Latin America: What Are the Key Issues for Practitioners?" Presented at the Darden Graduate School of Business Administration's "Valuation in Emerging Markets" conference. University of Virginia, May 2002.

Schramm, R., and H. Wang. 1999. "Measuring the Cost of Capital in an International CAPM Framework." *Journal of Applied Corporate Finance*, vol. 12, no. 3 (Fall):63–72.

Smith, Graham, Keith Jefferis, and Hyun-Jung Ryoo. 2002. "African Stock Markets: Multiple Variance Ratio Tests of Random Walks." *Applied Financial Economics*, vol. 12, no. 7:475–484.

Solnik, B. 1976. "L'Internationalisation des Places Financieres." Working paper, COB-Universite.

———. 1996. *International Investments*. 3rd ed. Reading, MA: Addison-Wesley.

Standard & Poor's. 2000. "The S&P Emerging Market Indices: Methodology, Definitions and Practices." (February). Available online at www2.standardand poors.com/spf/pdf/index/method.pdf.

———. 2002. *Emerging Stock Markets Factbook*. New York: McGraw-Hill.

Stulz, R. 1995. "Globalization of Capital Markets and the Cost of Capital: The Case of Nestle." *Journal of Applied Corporate Finance*, vol. 8, no. 3 (Fall):30–38.

———. 1999. "Globalization, Corporate Finance, and the Cost of Capital." *Journal of Applied Corporate Finance*, vol. 12, no. 3 (Fall):8–25.

Sy, Amadou. 2002. "Emerging Market Bond Spreads and Sovereign Credit Ratings: Reconciling Market Views with Economic Fundamentals." *Emerging Markets Review*, vol. 3, no. 4 (December):380–408.

Unro, Lee. 1997. "Stock Market and Macroeconomic Policies: New Evidence From Pacific Basin Countries." *Multinational Finance Journal*, vol. 1, no. 4:273–289.

Urrutia, Jorge, L. 1995. "Tests of Random Walk and Market Efficiency for Latin American Emerging Markets." *Journal of Financial Research*, vol. 18, no. 3:299–310.